Rich Dad's
CASHFLOW QUADRANT

Guide to Financial Freedom
By Robert T. Kiyosaki

Rich Dad's
CASHFLOW QUADRANT

Guide to Financial Freedom
By Robert T. Kiyosaki

PLATA™
PUBLISHING

Copyright © 2012 by CASHFLOW Technologies, Inc. All rights reserved. Except as permitted under the U.S. Copyright Act of 1976, no part of this publication may be reproduced, distributed, or transmitted in any form or by any means or stored in a database or retrieval system, without the prior written permission of the publisher.

Published by Plata Publishing, LLC

CASHFLOW, Rich Dad, Rich Dad Advisors, ESBI, and B-I Triangle are registered trademarks of CASHFLOW Technologies, Inc.

  are registered trademarks of
CASHFLOW Technologies, Inc.

Plata Publishing, LLC
4330 N. Civic Center Plaza
Suite 100
Scottsdale, AZ 85251
(480) 998-6971

Visit our websites: PlataPublishing.com and RichDad.com
Printed in the United States of America
052013

First Edition: 1998
First Plata Publishing Edition: 2011
ISBN: 978-1-61268-006-4
Cover photo credit: Seymour & Brody Studio

BEST-SELLING BOOKS
BY ROBERT T. KIYOSAKI

Rich Dad Poor Dad
What the Rich Teach Their Kids About Money –
That the Poor and Middle Class Do Not

Rich Dad's CASHFLOW Quadrant
Guide to Financial Freedom

Rich Dad's Guide to Investing
What the Rich Invest in That the Poor and Middle Class Do Not

Rich Dad's Rich Kid Smart Kid
Give Your Child a Financial Head Start

Rich Dad's Retire Young Retire Rich
How to Get Rich and Stay Rich

Rich Dad's Prophecy
Why the Biggest Stock Market Crash in History Is Still Coming...
And How You Can Prepare Yourself and Profit from It!

Rich Dad's Success Stories
Real-Life Success Stories from Real-Life People
Who Followed the Rich Dad Lessons

Rich Dad's Guide to Becoming Rich
Without Cutting Up Your Credit Cards
Turn Bad Debt into Good Debt

Rich Dad's Who Took My Money?
Why Slow Investors Lose and Fast Money Wins!

Rich Dad Poor Dad for Teens
The Secrets About Money – That You Don't Learn In School!

Escape the Rat Race
Learn How Money Works and Become a Rich Kid

Rich Dad's Before You Quit Your Job
Ten Real-Life Lessons Every Entrepreneur Should Know
About Building a Multimillion-Dollar Business

Rich Dad's Increase Your Financial IQ
Get Smarter with Your Money

Robert Kiyosaki's Conspiracy of the Rich
The 8 New Rules of Money

Unfair Advantage
The Power of Financial Education

Why "A" Students Work for "C" Students
Rich Dad's Guide to Financial Education for Parents

My rich dad used to say,
"You can never have true freedom without
financial freedom."

He would go on to say,
"Freedom may be free, but it has a price."

This book is dedicated to those who are
willing to pay the price.

Editor's Note

The Times They Are A-Changin'

There have been many changes in our economy and the investing landscape since *Rich Dad Poor Dad* was first published in 1997. Fourteen years ago, Robert Kiyosaki challenged conventional wisdom with his bold statement that "your house is not an asset." His contrarian views on money and investing were met with skepticism, criticism, and outrage.

In 2002, Robert's book, *Rich Dad's Prophecy*, advised that we prepare for an upcoming financial market crash. In 2006, Robert joined forces with Donald Trump to write *Why We Want You To Be Rich*, a book inspired by their concern for the shrinking middle class in America.

Robert continues to be a passionate advocate for the importance and power of financial education. Today, in the wake of the subprime fiasco, record home foreclosures, and a global economic meltdown that is still raging, his words seem not only prophetic, but enlightened. Many skeptics have become believers.

In preparing the 2011 edition of *Rich Dad's CASHFLOW Quadrant*, Robert realized two things: that his message and teachings have withstood the test of time, and that the investment landscape, the world in which investors operate, has changed dramatically. These changes have affected, and will continue to affect, those in the I (Investor) quadrant and have fueled Robert's decision to update an important section in this book—Chapter Five: The Five Levels of Investors.

Acknowledgments

The phenomenal success of *Rich Dad Poor Dad* has brought millions of new friends from all over the world.

Their kind words and friendship—and their amazing stories of perseverance, passion, and success in applying the Rich Dad principles to their lives—inspired me to write this book:

Rich Dad's CASHFLOW Quadrant
Guide to Financial Freedom

So to my friends, old and new, for their enthusiastic support beyond my wildest dreams, I say thank you.

Contents

Contents

WHAT IS YOUR LIFE'S GOAL?

"What do you want to be when you grow up?"
That is a question most of us have been asked.

I had many interests as a kid, and it was easy to
choose. If it sounded exciting and glamorous, I wanted
to do it. I wanted to be a marine biologist, an astronaut,
a Marine, a ship's officer, a pilot, and a professional
football player.

I was fortunate enough to achieve three of those
goals: a Marine Corps officer, a ship's officer, and a pilot.

I knew I did not want to become a teacher, a writer,
or an accountant. I did not want to be a teacher because
I did not like school. I did not want to be a writer
because I failed English twice. And I dropped out of my
MBA program because I could not stand accounting.

Ironically, now that I have grown up, I have become
everything I never wanted to become. Although I
disliked school, today I own an education company.
I personally teach around the world because I love
teaching. Although I failed English twice because I could
not write, today I am best known as an author. My
book, *Rich Dad Poor Dad*, was on the *New York Times*
best-sellers list for over seven years and is one of the top

three best-selling books in the United States. The only books ahead of it are *The Joy of Sex* and *The Road Less Traveled.* Adding one more irony, *Rich Dad Poor Dad* and my *CASHFLOW* board game are a book and a game about accounting, another subject I struggled with.

So what does this have to do with the question: "What is your goal in life?"

The answer is found in the simple, yet profound, statement by a Vietnamese monk, Thich Naht Hahn: "The path is the goal." In other words, finding your path in life is your goal in life. Your path is not your profession, how much money you make, your title, or your successes and failures.

Finding your path means finding out what you were put here on this earth to do. What is your life's purpose? Why were you given this gift called life? And what is the gift you give back to life?

Looking back, I know going to school was not about finding my life's path. I spent four years in military school, studying and training to be a ship's officer. If I had made a career sailing for Standard Oil on their oil tankers, I would never have found my life's path. If I had stayed in the Marines or had gone to fly for the airlines, I would never have found my life's path.

Had I continued on as a ship's officer or become an airline pilot, I would never have become an international best-selling author, been a guest on the *Oprah* show, written a book with Donald Trump, or started an international education company that teaches entrepreneurship and investing throughout the world.

Finding Your Path

This *CASHFLOW Quadrant* book is important because it is about finding your path in life. As you know, most people are programmed early in life to "Go to school and get a job." School is about finding a job in the E or S quadrant. It is not about finding your life's path.

I realize there are people who know exactly what they are going to do early in life. They grow up knowing they are going to be a doctor, lawyer, musician, golfer or actor. We have all heard about child prodigies, kids with exceptional talents. Yet you may notice, these are professions, not necessarily a life's path.

So How Does One Find Their Path in Life?

My answer is: I wish I knew. If I could wave my magic wand and your life's path would magically appear, I would.

Since I do not have a magic wand nor can I tell you what to do, the best thing I can do is tell you what I did. And what I did was trust my intuition, my heart, and my guts. For example, in 1973, returning from the war, when my poor dad suggested I go back to school, get my higher degrees, and work for the government, my brain went numb, my heart went heavy and my gut said, "No way."

When he suggested I get my old job back with Standard Oil or fly for the airlines, again my mind, heart, and gut said no. I knew I was through sailing and flying, although they were great professions and the pay was pretty good.

In 1973 at the age of 26, I was growing up. I had followed my parent's advice and gone to school, received my college degree, and had two professions: a license to be a ship's officer and a license to fly. The problem was, they were professions and the dreams of a child.

At the age of 26, I was old enough to know that education is a process. For example, when I wanted to be a ship's officer, I went to a school that turned out ships' officers. And when I wanted to learn to fly, I went to Navy flight school, a two-year process that turns non-pilots into pilots. I was cautious about my next educational process. I wanted to know what I was going to become before I started my next educational process.

Traditional schools had been good to me. I had achieved my childhood professions. Reaching adulthood was confusing because there were no signs saying, "This is the way." I knew what I *didn't* want to do, but I did not know what I *wanted* to do.

It would have been simple if all I wanted was a new profession. If I had wanted to be a medical doctor, I would have gone to medical school. If I had wanted to be a lawyer, I would have gone to law school. But I knew there was more to life than just going to school to gain another professional credential.

I did not realize it at the time, but at 26 years of age, I was now looking for my path in life, not my next profession.

A Different Education

In 1973, in my last year of active duty flying for the Marine Corps when I was stationed near home in Hawaii, I knew I wanted to follow in my rich dad's footsteps. While in the Marines, I signed up for real estate courses and business courses on the weekends, preparing to become an entrepreneur in the B and I quadrants.

At the same time, upon a friend's recommendation of a friend, I signed up for a personal-development course, hoping to find out who I really was. A personal-development course is non-traditional education because I was not taking it for credits or grades. I did not know what I was going to learn, as I did when I signed up for real estate courses. All I knew was that it was time to take courses to find out about me.

In my first weekend course, the instructor drew this simple diagram on the flip chart:

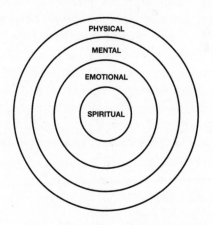

With the diagram complete, the instructor turned and said, "To develop into a whole human being, we need mental, physical, emotional, and spiritual education."

Listening to her explanation, it was clear to me that traditional schools were primarily about developing students mentally. That is why so many students who do well in school, do not do well in real life, especially in the world of money.

As the course progressed over the weekend, I discovered why I disliked school. I realized that I loved learning, but hated school.

Traditional education was a great environment for the "A" students, but it was not the environment for me. Traditional education was crushing my spirit, trying to motivate me with the emotion of fear: the fear of making mistakes, the fear of failing, and the fear of not getting a job. They were programming me to be an employee in the E or S quadrant. I realized that traditional education is not the place for a person who wants to be an entrepreneur in the B and I quadrants.

This may be why so many entrepreneurs never finish school—entrepreneurs like Thomas Edison, founder of General Electric; Henry Ford, founder of Ford Motor Company; Steve Jobs, founder of Apple; Bill Gates, founder of Microsoft; Walt Disney, founder of Disneyland; and Mark Zuckerberg, founder of Facebook.

As the day went on and the instructor went deeper and deeper into these four types of personal development, I realized I had spent most of my life in very harsh educational environments. After four years at an all-male military academy and five years as a Marine pilot, I was pretty strong mentally and physically. As a Marine pilot, I was strong emotionally and spiritually, but all on the macho-male development side. I had no gentle side, no female energy. After all, I was trained to be Marine Corps officer, emotionally calm under pressure, prepared to kill, and spiritually prepared to die for my country.

If you ever saw the movie "Top Gun" starring Tom Cruise, you get a glimpse into the masculine world and bravado of military pilots. I loved that world. I was good in that world. It was a modern-day world of knights and warriors. It was not a world for wimps.

In the seminar, I went into my emotions and briefly touched my spirit. I cried a lot because I had a lot to cry about. I had done and seen things no one should ever be asked to do. During the seminar, I hugged a man, something I had never done before, not even with my father.

On Sunday night, it was difficult leaving this self-development workshop. The seminar had been a gentle, loving, honest environment. Monday morning was a shock to once again be surrounded by young egotistical pilots, dedicated to flying, killing and dying for country.

After that weekend seminar, I knew it was time to change. I knew developing myself emotionally and spiritually to become a kinder, gentler, and more compassionate person would be the hardest thing I could do. It went against all my years at the military academy and flight school.

I never returned to traditional education again. I had no desire to study for grades, degrees, promotions, or credentials again. From then on, if I did attend a course or school, I went to learn, to become a better person. I was no longer in the paper chase of grades, degrees, and credentials.

Growing up in a family of teachers, your grades, the high school and college you graduated from, and your advanced degrees were everything. Like the medals and ribbons on a Marine pilot's chest, advanced degrees and brand-name schools were the status and the stripes that educators wore on their sleeves. In their minds, people who did not finish high school were the unwashed, the lost souls of life. Those with master's degrees looked down on those with only bachelor degrees. Those with a PhD were held in reverence. At the age of 26, I knew I would never return to that world.

Editor's Note: In 2009, Robert received an honorary PhD in entrepreneurship from prestigious San Ignacio de Loyola in Lima, Peru. The few other recipients of this award are political leaders, such as the former President of Spain.

Finding My Path

I know some of you are now asking: Why is he spending so much time talking about non-traditional education courses?

The reason is, that first personal-development seminar rekindled my love of learning, but not the type of learning that is taught in school. Once that seminar was over, I became a seminar junkie, going from seminar to seminar, finding out more about the connection between *my* body, *my* mind, *my* emotions, and *my* spirit.

The more I studied, the more curious about traditional education I became. I began to ask questions such as:

- Why do so many kids hate school?

- Why do so few kids like school?

- Why are many highly educated people not successful in the real world?

- Does school prepare you for the real world?

- Why did I hate school but love learning?

- Why are most schoolteachers poor?

- Why do schools teach us little about money?

Those questions led me to become a student of education outside the hallowed walls of the school system. The more I studied, the more I understood why I did not like school and why schools failed to serve most of its students, even the "A" students.

My curiosity touched my spirit, and I became an entrepreneur in education. If not for this curiosity, I might never have become an author and a developer of financial-education games. My spiritual education led me to my path in life.

It seems that our paths in life are not found in our minds. Our path in life is to find out what is in our hearts.

This does not mean a person cannot find their path in traditional education. I am sure many do. I am just saying that I doubt I would have found my path in traditional school.

Why Is a Path Important?

We all know people who make a lot of money, but hate their work. We also know people who do not make a lot of money and hate their work. And we all know people who just work for money.

A classmate of mine from the Merchant Marine Academy also realized he did not want to spend his life at sea. Rather than sail for the rest of his life, he went to law school after graduation, spending three more years becoming a lawyer and entering private practice in the S quadrant.

He died in his early fifties. He had become a very successful, unhappy lawyer. Like me, he had two professions by the time he was 26. Although he hated being a lawyer, he continued being a lawyer because he had a family, kids, a mortgage, and bills to pay.

A year before he died, I met him at a class reunion in New York. He was a bitter man. "All I do is sweep up behind rich guys like you. They pay me nothing. I hate what I do and who I work for."

"Why don't you do something else?" I asked.

"I can't afford to stop working. My first child is entering college."

He died of a heart attack before she graduated.

He made a lot of money via his professional training, but he was emotionally angry, spiritually dead, and soon his body followed.

I realize this is an extreme example. Most people do not hate what they do as much as my friend did. Yet it illustrates the problem when a person is trapped in a profession and unable to find their path.

To me, this is the shortcoming of traditional education. Millions of people leave school, only to be trapped in jobs they do not like. They know something is missing in life. Many people are also trapped financially, earning just enough to survive, wanting to earn more but not knowing what to do.

Without awareness of the other quadrants, many people go back to school and look for new professions or pay raises in the E or S quadrant, unaware of the world of the B and I quadrants.

My Reason for Becoming a Teacher

My primary reason for becoming a teacher in the B quadrant was a desire to provide financial education. I wanted to make this education available to anyone who wanted to learn, regardless of how much money they had or what their grade-point averages were. That is why The Rich Dad Company started with the *CASHFLOW* game. This game can teach in places I could never go. The beauty of the game is that it was designed to have people teach people. There is no need for an expensive teacher or classroom. The *CASHFLOW* game is now translated into over sixteen languages, reaching millions of people all over the world.

Today, The Rich Dad Company offers financial-education courses as well as the services of coaches and mentors to support a person's financial education. Our programs are especially important for anyone wanting to evolve out of the E and S quadrants into the B and I quadrants.

There is no guarantee that everyone will make it to the B and I quadrants, yet they will know how to access those quadrants if they want to.

Change Is Not Easy

For me, changing quadrants was not easy. It was hard work mentally, but more so emotionally and spiritually. Growing up in a family of highly educated employees in the E quadrant, I carried their values of education, job security, benefits, and a government pension. In many ways, my family values made my transition difficult. I had to shut out their warnings, concerns, and criticisms about becoming an entrepreneur and investor.

Some of their values I had to discount were:

- "But you have to have a job."

- "You're taking too many risks."

- "What if you fail?"

- "Just go back to school and get your masters degree."

- "Become a doctor. They make a lot of money."

- "The rich are greedy."

- "Why is money so important to you?"

- "Money won't make you happy."

- "Just live below your means."

- "Play it safe. Don't go for your dreams."

Diet and Exercise

I mention emotional and spiritual development because that is what it takes to make a permanent change in life. For example, it rarely works to tell an overweight person, "Just eat less and exercise more." Diet and exercise may make sense mentally, but most people who are overweight do not eat because they are hungry. They eat to feed an emptiness in their emotions and their soul. When a person goes on a diet-and-exercise program, they are only working on their mind and their body. Without emotional development and spiritual strength, the overweight person may go on a diet for six months and lose a ton of weight, only to put even more weight back on later.

The same is true for changing quadrants. Saying to yourself, "I'm going to become an entrepreneur in the B quadrant," is as futile as a chain smoker saying, "Tomorrow I'm going to quit smoking." Smoking is a physical addiction caused by emotional and spiritual challenges. Without emotional and spiritual support, the smoker will always be a smoker. The same is true for an alcoholic, a sex addict, or a chronic shopper. Most addictions are attempts to find happiness in people's souls.

This is why my company offers courses for the mind and body, but also coaches and mentors to support the emotional and spiritual transitions.

A few people are able to make the journey alone, but I was not one of them. If not for a coach like my rich dad and the support of my wife Kim, I would not have made it. There were so many times I wanted to quit and give up. If not for Kim and my rich dad, I would have quit.

Why "A" Students Fail

Looking at the diagram again, it is easy to see why so many "A" students fail in the world of money.

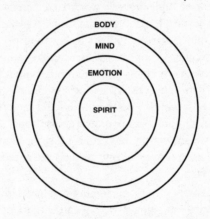

A person may be highly educated mentally, but if they are not educated emotionally, their fear will often stop their body from doing what it must do. That is why so many "A" students get stuck in "analysis paralysis," studying every little detail, but failing to do anything.

This "analysis paralysis" is caused by our educational system punishing students for making mistakes. If you think about it, "A" students are "A" students simply because they made the fewest mistakes. The problem with that emotional psychosis is that, in the real world, people who take action are the ones who make the most mistakes and learn from them to win in the game of life.

Just look at Presidents Clinton and Bush. Clinton could not admit he had sex and Bush II could not recall any mistakes he made during his presidency. Making mistakes is human, but lying about your mistakes is criminal, a criminal act known as perjury.

When criticized for making 1,014 mistakes before creating the electric light bulb, Thomas Edison said, "I did not fail 1,014 times. I successfully found out what did not work 1,014 times."

In other words, the reason so many people fail to achieve success is because they fail to fail enough times.

Looking at the diagram again,

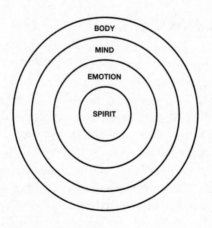

one of the reasons so many people cling to job security is because they lack emotional education. They let fear stop them.

One of the best things about military school and the Marine Corps is that these organizations spend a lot of time developing young men and women spiritually, emotionally, mentally, and physically. Although it was a tough education, it was a complete education, preparing us to do a nasty job.

The reason I created the *CASHFLOW* game is because the game educates the whole person. The game is a better teaching tool than reading or lecture, simply because the game involves the body, mind, emotions, and spirit of the player.

The game is designed for players to make as many mistakes as possible with play money, and then learn from those mistakes. To me, this is a more humane way to learn about money.

The Path Is the Goal

Today, there are thousands of CASHFLOW clubs all over the world. One reason why CASHFLOW clubs are important is because they are a shelter from the storm, a way station on the path of life. By joining a CASHFLOW club, you get to meet people like you, people who are committed to making changes, not just talking about change.

Unlike school, there is not a requirement of past academic success. All that is asked is a sincere desire to learn and make changes. In the game, you will make a lot of mistakes in different financial situations and will learn from your mistakes, using play money.

CASHFLOW clubs are not for those who want to get rich quick. CASHFLOW clubs are there to support the long-term mental, emotional, spiritual, physical, and financial changes a person needs to go through. We all change and evolve at different rates of speed so you are encouraged to go at your own speed.

After playing the game with others a few times, you will have a better idea of what your next step should be and which of the four asset classes (business, real estate, paper assets, or commodities) is best for you.

In Conclusion

Finding one's path is not necessarily easy. Even today, I do not really know if I am on my path or not. As you know, we all get lost at times, and it is not always easy to find our way back.

If you feel you are not in the right quadrant for you, or you are not on your life's path, I encourage you to search your heart and find your path in life. You may know it is time to change if you are saying things like the following statements:

- "I'm working with dead people."

- "I love what I do, but I wish I could make more money."

- "I can't wait for the weekend."

- "I want to do my own thing."

- "Is it quitting time yet?"

My sister is a Buddhist nun. Her path is to support the Dalai Lama, a path that pays nothing. Yet, although she earns little, it does not mean she has to be a poor nun. She has her own rental property and investments in gold and silver. Her strength of spirit and her financially educated mind allow her to follow her life's path without taking a vow of poverty.

In many ways, it was a good thing I was labeled stupid in school. Although emotionally painful, that pain allowed me to find my life's path as a teacher. And like my sister, the nun, just because I am a teacher does not mean I have to be a poor teacher.

Repeating what Thich Naht Hahn said: "The path is the goal."

Introduction
WHICH QUADRANT ARE YOU IN?

*The CASHFLOW Quadrant®
is a way to categorize people
based on where their money comes from.*

Are you financially free? If your life has come to a financial fork in the road, *Rich Dad's CASHFLOW Quadrant* was written for you. If you want to take control of what you do today in order to change your financial destiny, this book will help you chart your course.

This is the CASHFLOW Quadrant. The letters in each quadrant represent:

E for employee
S for small business or self-employed
B for big business (500 employees)
I for investor

Each of us resides in at least one of the four sections (quadrants) of the CASHFLOW Quadrant. Where we are is determined by where our cash comes from. Many of us are employees who rely on paychecks, while others are self-employed. Employees and self-employed individuals reside on the left side of the CASHFLOW Quadrant. The right side is for individuals who receive their cash from businesses they own or investments they own.

The CASHFLOW Quadrant is an easy way to categorize people based on where their money comes from. Each quadrant within the CASHFLOW Quadrant is unique, and the people within each one share common characteristics. The quadrants will show you where you are today and will help you chart a course for where you want to be in the future as you choose your own path to financial freedom. While financial freedom can be found in all four of the quadrants, the skills of a B or I will help you reach your financial goals more quickly. Successful E's need to become successful I's to ensure their financial security during retirement.

What Do You Want to Be When You Grow Up?

This book is, in many ways, Part II of my book, *Rich Dad Poor Dad*. For those of you who may not have read *Rich Dad Poor Dad,* it is about the different lessons my two dads taught me about money and life choices. One was my real dad, and the other was my best friend's dad. One was highly educated and the other was a high school dropout. One was poor, and the other was rich.

Poor Dad's Advice

Growing up, my highly educated, but poor, dad always said, "Go to school, get good grades, and find a safe secure job." He was recommending a life path that looked like this:

Poor dad recommended that I become either a well-paid E, employee, or a well-paid S, self-employed professional, such as a medical doctor, lawyer, or accountant. My poor dad was very concerned about a steady paycheck, benefits, and job security. That's why he was a well-paid government official, the head of education for the State of Hawaii.

Rich Dad's Advice

My rich, but uneducated, dad offered very different advice. He said, "Go to school, graduate, build businesses, and become a successful investor." He was recommending a life path that looked like this:

This book is about the mental, emotional, and educational process I went through in following my rich dad's advice.

Who Is This Book For?

This book is written for people who are ready to change quadrants, especially for individuals who are currently in the E and S categories and are contemplating moving to the B or I category. This book is for people who are ready to move beyond job security and begin to achieve financial security. It's not an easy life path, but the prize at the end of the road, financial freedom, is worth the journey.

When I was 12 years old, rich dad told me a simple story that guided me to great wealth and financial freedom. It was his way of explaining the difference between the left side of the CASHFLOW Quadrant, the E and S quadrants, and the right side, or the B and I quadrants. The story goes like this:

"Once upon a time there was this quaint little village. It was a great place to live except for one problem. The village had no water unless it rained. To solve this problem once and for all, the village elders asked contractors to submit bids to deliver water to the village on a daily basis. Two people volunteered to take on the task, and the elders awarded the contract to both of them. They felt that a little competition would keep prices low and ensure a backup supply of water.

"The first person who won the contract, Ed, immediately ran out, bought two galvanized steel buckets and began running back and forth to the lake which was a mile away. He immediately began making money as he labored morning to dusk, hauling water from the lake with his two buckets. He would empty them into the large concrete holding tank the village had built. Each morning he had to get up before the rest of the village awoke to make sure there was enough water for the people. It was hard work, but he was very happy to be making money and for having one of the two exclusive contracts for this business.

"The second winning contractor, Bill, disappeared for a while. He wasn't seen for months, which made Ed very happy, since he had no competition.

"Instead of buying two buckets to compete with Ed, Bill wrote a business plan, created a corporation, found four investors, employed a president to do the work, and returned six months later with a construction crew. Within a year, his team had built a large-volume stainless-steel pipeline which connected the village to the lake.

"At the grand-opening celebration, Bill announced that his water was cleaner than Ed's water. Bill knew that the villagers had complained about the water's lack of cleanliness. Bill also announced that he could supply the village with water 24 hours a day, 7 days a week. Ed could only deliver water on weekdays because he didn't want to work on weekends. Then Bill announced that he would charge 75 percent less than Ed did for this higher-quality, more-reliable water. The villagers cheered and immediately ran for the faucet at the end of Bill's pipeline.

"In order to compete, Ed immediately lowered his rates by 75 percent, bought two more buckets, added covers to his buckets and began hauling four buckets each trip. In order to provide better service, he hired his two sons to give him a hand on the night shift and on weekends. When his boys went off to college, he said to them, 'Hurry back because someday this business will belong to you.'

"For some reason, his two sons never returned. Eventually, Ed had employees and union problems. The union demanded higher wages and better benefits and wanted its members to only haul one bucket at a time.

"Meanwhile, Bill realized that if this village needed water, then other villages must need water too. He rewrote his business plan and went off to sell his high-speed, high-volume, low-cost, clean-water delivery system to villages throughout the world. He only makes a penny per bucket of water delivered, but he delivers billions of buckets of water every day. Whether he works or not, billions of people consume billions of buckets of water, and all that money pours into his bank account. Bill developed a pipeline to deliver money to himself, as well as water to the villages.

"Bill lived happily ever after. Ed worked hard for the rest of his life and had financial problems forever after. The end."

That story about Bill and Ed has guided me for years. It has assisted me in my life's decision-making process. I often ask myself:

"Am I building a pipeline or hauling buckets?"

"Am I working hard, or am I working smart?"

And the answers to those questions have made me financially free.

That is what this book is about. It's about what it takes to become a B and an I. It's for people who are tired of hauling buckets and are ready to build pipelines for cash to flow into their pockets.

This Book Is Divided into Three Parts

Part I The first part of this book focuses on the core differences between people in the four quadrants. It shows why certain people gravitate to certain quadrants and often get stuck there without realizing it. It will help you identify where you are today in the quadrant and where you want to be in five years.

Part II The second part of this book is about personal change. It's more about who you have to be, instead of what you have to do.

Part III The third part of this book explains how to find success on the right side of the CASHFLOW Quadrant. I will share more of my rich dad's secrets on the skills required to be a successful B and I. It will help you choose your own path to financial freedom.

Throughout *Rich Dad's CASHFLOW Quadrant,* I continue to stress the importance of financial intelligence. If you want to operate on the right side, the B- and I-quadrant side, you must be smarter than if you choose to stay on the left side, the E- and S-quadrant side. To be a B or I, you must be able to control the direction of your cash flow.

This book is written for people who are ready to make changes in their lives to move beyond job security and begin to build their own pipelines to achieve financial freedom.

We are in the Information Age which offers more opportunities for financial reward than ever before. Individuals with the skills of the B's and I's will be able to identify and seize those opportunities. To be successful in the Information Age, a person needs information from all four quadrants. Unfortunately, our schools are still in the Industrial Age and still prepare students for only the left side of the CASHFLOW Quadrant.

If you're looking for new answers to move forward in the Information Age, this book is for you. It doesn't have all the answers, but it will share the deep personal and guiding insights I gained as I traveled from the E and S side to the B and I side.

THE CASHFLOW QUADRANT

Chapter One
WHY DON'T YOU
GET A JOB?

---

*To someone who values a job, it's difficult to explain
why you might not want one.*

In 1985, my wife Kim and I were homeless. We
were unemployed and had little money left in savings.
Our credit cards were exhausted, and we lived in an
old brown Toyota with reclining seats that served as
beds. At the end of one week, the harsh reality of who
we were, what we were doing, and where we were
headed began to sink in.

Our homelessness lasted another two weeks. When
a friend realized our desperate financial situation, she
offered us a room in her basement. We lived there for
nine months.

We kept our situation quiet. For the most part,
Kim and I looked quite normal on the surface. When
friends and family were informed of our plight, the
first question was always, "Why don't you get a job?"

At first, we attempted to explain, but we usually
failed to clarify our reasons. To someone who values

a job, it's difficult to explain why you might not want one.

We did odd jobs occasionally and earned a few dollars here and there, but we did that only to keep food in our stomachs and gas in the car. Those few extra dollars were only fuel to keep us going toward our singular goal. I must admit that during moments of deep personal doubt, the idea of a safe, secure job with a paycheck was appealing.

But because job security wasn't what we were looking for, we kept pushing on, living day to day, on the brink of the financial abyss.

That year, 1985, was the worst of our lives as well as one of the longest. Anyone who says that money isn't important obviously has not been without it for long. Kim and I fought and argued often. Fear, uncertainty, and hunger shortens the human emotional fuse, and often we fight with the person who loves us the most. Yet love held the two of us together, and our bond as a couple grew stronger because of the adversity. We knew where we were going. We just didn't know if we would ever get there.

We knew we could always find safe, secure, high-paying jobs. Both of us were college graduates with good job skills and solid work ethics. But we weren't after job security. We wanted financial freedom.

By 1989, we were millionaires. Although financially successful in some people's eyes, we still hadn't reached our goal of true financial freedom. That took until 1994. By then, we never had to work again for the rest of our lives. Barring any unforeseen financial disaster, we were both financially free. Kim was 37 and I was 47.

It Doesn't Take Money to Make Money

I started this chapter with a discussion about our being homeless and having nothing in 1985 because I often hear people say, "It takes money to make money."

I disagree. To get from homeless in 1985, to rich in 1989, and then to financial freedom by 1994, didn't take money. We had no money when we started, and we were in debt.

It also doesn't take a good formal education. I have a college degree, and I can honestly say that achieving financial freedom had nothing to do with what I learned in college. I didn't find much demand for my years of studying calculus, spherical trigonometry, chemistry, physics, French, and English literature.

Many successful people have left school without receiving a college degree—people such as Thomas Edison, founder of General Electric; Henry Ford, founder of Ford Motor Co.; Bill Gates, founder of Microsoft; Ted Turner, founder of CNN; Michael Dell, founder of Dell Computers; Steve Jobs, founder of Apple Computer; and Ralph Lauren, founder of Polo. A college education is important for traditional professions, but not for how these people found great wealth. They developed their own successful businesses, and that was what Kim and I were striving for.

So What Does It Take?

I am often asked, "If it doesn't take money to make money, and schools don't teach you how to become financially free, then what does it take?"

My answer: It takes a dream, a lot of determination, a willingness to learn quickly, and the ability to use your God-given assets properly and to know which quadrant in the CASHFLOW Quadrant is the right one for you to generate your income.

What Is the CASHFLOW Quadrant?

The diagram below is the CASHFLOW Quadrant. The letters in each quadrant represent:

E for employee
S for small business or self-employed
B for big business (500 employees)
I for investor

From Which Quadrant Do You Generate Your Income?

The CASHFLOW Quadrant represents the different methods by which income or money is generated. For example, an employee earns money by holding a job and working for a person or a company. Self-employed people earn money working for themselves. A business owner owns a business that generates money, and investors earn money from their various investments—in other words, money generating more money.

Different methods of income generation require different frames of mind, different technical skills, and different educational paths. Different people are attracted to different quadrants.

While money is all the same, the way it's earned can be vastly different. If you begin to look at the four different labels for each quadrant, you might want to ask yourself, "Which quadrant do I generate the majority of my income from?"

Each quadrant is different. To generate income from different quadrants requires different skills and a different personality, even if the person found in each quadrant is the same. Changing from quadrant to quadrant is like playing golf in the morning and then attending the ballet at night.

You Can Earn Income in All Four Quadrants

Most of us have the potential to generate income from all four quadrants. Which quadrant you or I choose to earn our primary income from is not so much dependent upon what we learned in school. It's more about who we are at the core—our values, strengths, weaknesses, and interests. These core differences attract us to, or repel us from, each quadrant.

Yet, regardless of what type of work we perform, we can still work in all four quadrants. For example, a medical doctor could choose to earn income as an E and join the staff of a large hospital or an insurance company, work for the government in the public-health field, or become a military doctor.

This same doctor could also decide to earn income as an S and start a private practice, setting up an office, hiring staff, and building a private list of patients.

Or the doctor could decide to become a B and own a clinic or laboratory and have other doctors on staff. This doctor probably would hire a business manager to run the organization. In this case, the doctor would own the business but not have to work in it. The doctor also could decide to own a business that has nothing to do with the medical field while still practicing medicine somewhere else. In this case, the doctor would be earning income as both an E and as a B.

As an I, the doctor could generate income from being an investor in someone else's business or in vehicles like the stock market, bond market, and real estate.

The important words are "generate income from." It's not so much what we do, but more how we generate income.

Different Methods of Income Generation

More than anything, it's the internal differences of our core values, strengths, weaknesses, and interests that affect which quadrant we decide to generate our income from. Some people love being employees, while others hate it. Some people love owning companies but don't want to run them. Others love owning companies and also love running them. Some people love investing, while others can't get past the risk of losing money. Most of us are a little of each of these characters. Being successful in the four quadrants often means redirecting some internal core values.

You Can Be Rich or Poor in All Four Quadrants

It is important to note that you can be rich or poor in all four quadrants. There are people who earn millions and people who go bankrupt in each of the quadrants. Being in one quadrant or another does not necessarily guarantee financial success.

Not All Quadrants Are Equal

By knowing the different features of each quadrant, you'll have a better idea as to which quadrant, or quadrants, might be best for you.

For example, one of the many reasons I chose to work predominantly in the B and I quadrants is because of tax advantages. For most people working on the left side of the quadrant, there are few legal tax breaks available. Yet legal tax breaks abound on the right side of the quadrant. By working to generate income in the

B and I quadrants, I could acquire money faster and keep that money working for me longer without losing large chunks of it to the government in the form of taxes.

Different Ways of Earning Money

When people ask why Kim and I were homeless, I tell them it was because of what my rich dad taught me about money. For me, money is important, yet I didn't want to spend my life working for it. That is why I didn't want a job. If we were going to be responsible citizens, Kim and I wanted to have our money work for us, rather than spend our lives physically working for money.

That is why the CASHFLOW Quadrant is important. It depicts the different ways money is generated. There are ways of being responsible and creating money other than physically working for it.

Different Fathers—
Different Ideas about Money

My highly educated dad had a strong belief that the love of money was evil and that excessive profit meant you were greedy. He felt embarrassed when the newspapers published how much he made because he felt he was overcompensated in comparison to the teachers who worked for him. He was a good, honest, hardworking man who did his best to defend his point of view that money wasn't important to his life.

My highly educated, yet poor, dad constantly said,

- "I'm not that interested in money."

- "I'll never be rich."

- "I can't afford it."

- "Investing is risky."

- "Money isn't everything."

Money Supports Life

My rich dad had a different point of view. He thought it foolish to spend your life working for money and to pretend that money wasn't important. Rich dad believed that life was more important than money, but that money was important for supporting life. He often said, "You only have so many hours in a day, and you can only work so hard. So why work hard for money? Learn to have money and people work hard for you, and you can be free to do the things that are important." To my rich dad, what was important was:

- Having lots of time to raise his kids.

- Having money to donate to charities and projects he supported.

- Bringing jobs and financial stability to the community.

- Having time and money to take care of his health.

- Being able to travel the world with his family.

"Those things take money," said rich dad. "That's why money is important to me. Money is important, but I don't want to spend my life working for it."

Choosing Quadrants

One reason Kim and I focused on the B and I quadrants while we were homeless was because I had more training and education in those quadrants. It was because of my rich dad's guidance that I knew the different financial and professional advantages of each quadrant. For me, the quadrants on the right side, the B and I quadrants, offered the best opportunity for long-term financial success and financial freedom. Also, at age 37, I had experienced successes and failures in all four quadrants which allowed me some degree of understanding about my own personal temperament, likes, dislikes, strengths, and weaknesses. I knew which quadrants I did best in.

Parents Are Teachers

When I was a young boy, my rich dad often referred to the CASHFLOW Quadrant. He would explain to me the difference between someone who was successful on the left side versus the right side. But being young, I really didn't pay much attention to what he said. I didn't understand the difference between an employee's mindset and a business owner's mindset. I was just trying to survive school.

Yet I did hear his words, and soon they began to make sense. Having two dynamic and successful father figures around me gave meaning to what each was saying. But it was what they were doing that allowed me to begin to notice the differences between the E-S side and the B-I side. At first, the differences were subtle. Then they became glaring.

For example, one painful lesson I learned as a young boy was simply how much time one dad had available to spend with me versus the other. As the success and prominence of both dads grew, it was obvious that one dad had less and less time to spend with his wife and four children. My real dad was always on the road, at meetings, or dashing off to the airport for more meetings. The more successful he got, the fewer dinners we had together as a family. On weekends, he was at home in his crowded little office, buried under paperwork.

On the other hand, my rich dad had more and more free time as his success grew. One of the reasons I learned so much about money, finance, business, and life was simply because my rich dad had more and more free time for his children and me.

Another example is that both dads made more and more money as they became successful, but my real dad, the educated one, also got further into debt. So he'd work harder and suddenly find himself in a higher income-tax bracket. His banker and accountant would then tell him to buy a bigger house for the so-called "tax break." My dad would follow the advice and buy a bigger house, and soon he was working harder than ever so he could make more money to pay for it. Ultimately, this just took him even further away from his family.

My rich dad was different. He made more and more money but paid less in taxes. He also had bankers and accountants, but he wasn't getting the same advice my highly educated dad was getting.

The Main Reason

The driving force, however, that wouldn't allow me to stay on the left side of the Quadrant was what happened to my highly educated but poor dad at the peak of his career.

In the early 1970s, I was already out of college and in Pensacola, Florida, going through pilot training for the Marine Corps before a tour in Vietnam. My educated dad was now the superintendent of education for the State of Hawaii and a member of the governor's staff. One evening, he phoned me with some interesting news.

"Son," he said, "I'm going to resign from my job and run for lieutenant governor of Hawaii for the Republican party."

I gulped and then said, "You're going to run for office against your boss?"

"That's right," he replied.

"Why?" I asked. "Republicans don't have a chance in Hawaii. The Democratic party and the labor unions are too strong."

"I know, Son. I know that we don't have a prayer of winning. Judge Samuel King will be the candidate for governor, and I will be his running mate."

"Why?" I asked again. "Why go against your boss if you know you're going to lose?"

"Because my conscience won't let me do anything else. The games these politicians are playing disturb me."

"Are you saying they're corrupt?" I asked.

"I don't want to say that," said my real dad. He was an honest and moral man who rarely spoke badly about anyone. Yet I could tell from his voice that he was angry and upset when he said, "I'll just say that my conscience bothers me when I see what goes on behind the scenes. I couldn't live with myself if I turned a blind eye and did nothing. My job and paycheck aren't as important as my conscience."

After a long silence, I realized that my dad's mind was made up. "Good luck," I said quietly. "I'm proud of you for your courage, and I'm proud to be your son."

My dad and the Republican ticket were crushed, as expected. The re-elected governor sent the word out that my dad was never to work again for the State of Hawaii, and he never did. At the age of 54, my dad went looking for a job, and I was on my way to Vietnam.

When he was middle-aged, my dad was hunting for a job. He went from jobs with big titles and low pay to other jobs with big titles and low pay. He was a tall, brilliant, and dynamic man who was no longer welcome in the only world he knew, the world of government employees. He tried starting several small businesses. He was a consultant for a while and even bought a famous franchise, but all his efforts failed.

As he grew older and his strength slipped away, so did his drive to start over again. His lack of will became even more pronounced after each business failure. He was a successful E trying to survive as an S, a quadrant in which he had no training or experience and for which he had no heart. He loved the world of public education, but he couldn't find a way to get back in. The ban on his employment in the state government was silently, but firmly, in place.

If not for Social Security and Medicare, the last years of his life would have been a complete disaster. He died frustrated and a little angry, yet he died with a clear conscience.

So what kept me going in the darkest of hours? It was the haunting memory of my educated dad sitting at home, waiting for the phone to ring, trying to succeed in the world of business, a world he knew nothing about. That, and the joyous memory of seeing my rich dad grow happier and more successful as his years went on, inspired me.

Instead of declining at age 54, rich dad blossomed. He had become rich years before that, but now he was becoming mega-rich. He was constantly in the newspapers as the man who was buying up Waikiki and Maui. His years of methodically building businesses and investing were paying off, and he was on his way to becoming one of the richest men in the Islands.

Small Differences Become Large Differences

Because my rich dad had explained the quadrants to me, I was better able to see that small differences grow into large differences when measured over the years a person spends working. Because of the CASHFLOW Quadrant, I knew it was better to decide, not so much what I wanted to do, but more who I wanted to become as my working years progressed. In the darkest hours, it was this deep knowledge, and the lessons from two powerful dads, that kept me going.

It Is More Than the Quadrant

The CASHFLOW Quadrant is more than two lines and some letters. If you look below the surface of this simple diagram, you will find completely different worlds, as well as different ways of looking at the world. As a person who has looked at the world from both the left and the right sides, I can honestly say the world looks much different depending on which side you are on.

One quadrant is not better than another. Each has strengths and each has weaknesses. This book is written to give you a glimpse into the different quadrants and into the personal development required to be financially successful in each of them. It's my belief that you'll gain further insights into choosing the financial life path that's best suited for you.

Many of the skills essential to being successful on the right side of the quadrant aren't taught in school, which may explain how people like Bill Gates, Ted Turner, and Thomas Edison left school early and yet learned how to be successful B's and I's. This book will identify the skills, as well as the personal core temperament, that are necessary for finding success on the B and I side. First, I offer a broad overview of the four quadrants, and then an in-depth focus on the B and I side.

After reading this book, some of you might want to make a change in how you earn your income, and some of you will be happy to stay just where you are. You might choose to operate in more than one quadrant, maybe even in all four quadrants. We're all different, and one quadrant isn't more important or better than another. In every village, town, city, and nation in the world, there is a need for people to operate in all four quadrants in order to ensure the financial stability of the community.

Also, as we grow older and gain different experiences, our interests change. For example, I notice that many young people right out of school are often happy to get a job. But after a couple of years, a few of them decide they aren't interested in climbing the corporate ladder, or they lose interest in their chosen field. These changes of age and experience often cause a person to search for new avenues of growth, challenge, financial reward, and personal happiness. I hope this book offers some fresh ideas for attaining those goals.

In short, this book isn't about homelessness, but about finding a home—a home in a quadrant or quadrants.

Chapter Two
DIFFERENT QUADRANTS, DIFFERENT PEOPLE

---

*Changing quadrants is often
a change at the core of who you are.*

"You can't teach an old dog new tricks," my highly educated dad always said.

I had talked with him on several occasions, doing my best to explain the CASHFLOW Quadrant, in an effort to give him some new financial direction. Nearing 60 years of age, he was realizing that many of his dreams weren't going to be fulfilled. His "blacklisting" seemed to go beyond the walls of state government. He was now blacklisting himself.

"I tried it, but it didn't work," he said.

My dad was referring to his attempts to be successful in the S quadrant as a self-employed consultant, and as a B when he poured much of his life savings into a famous ice-cream franchise that failed.

Being bright, he conceptually understood the different technical skills required in each of the four quadrants. He knew he could learn them if he wanted to. But there was something else holding him back.

One day over lunch, I talked to my rich dad about my educated dad. "Your father and I aren't the same people at the core," said rich dad. "While we both have fears, doubts, beliefs, strengths, and weaknesses, we respond or handle those core similarities quite differently."

"Can you tell me the differences?" I asked.

"Not over one lunch," said rich dad. "But how we respond to those differences is what causes us to remain in one quadrant or another. When your dad tried to cross over from the E quadrant to the B quadrant, intellectually he could understand the process, but he couldn't handle it emotionally. When things didn't go smoothly and he began to lose money, he didn't know what to do to solve the problems, so he went back to the quadrant he felt most comfortable in."

"The E and sometimes S quadrant," I said.

Rich dad nodded his head. "When the fear of losing money and failing becomes too painful inside, a fear we both have, he chooses to seek security and I choose to seek freedom."

"And that is the core difference," I said, signaling the waiter for our check.

"Even though we're all human beings," said rich dad, "when it comes to money and the emotions attached to money, we all respond differently. And it's how we respond to those emotions that often determines which quadrant we choose to generate our income from."

"Different quadrants for different people," I said.

"That's right," said rich dad as we stood and headed for the door. "And if you're going to be successful in any quadrant, you need to have more than just technical skills. You also need to know the core differences that cause people to seek different quadrants. Know that, and life will be much easier."

We were shaking hands and saying good-bye as the valet brought my rich dad's car around.

"Oh, one last thing," I said hurriedly. "Can my dad change?"

"Oh sure," said rich dad. "Anyone can change. But changing quadrants isn't like changing jobs or changing professions. Changing quadrants is often a change at the core of who you are—how you think and how you look at the world. The change is easier for some people than for others simply because some people welcome change and others fight it. And changing quadrants is most often a life-changing experience. It's a change as profound as the age-old story of the caterpillar becoming a butterfly. Not only will you change, but so will your friends. While you'll still be friends with your old friends, it's just harder for caterpillars to do the same things butterflies do. So the changes are big changes, and not too many people choose to make them."

The valet closed the door, and as my rich dad drove off, I was left thinking about the core differences.

What Are the Core Differences?

How do I tell if people are an E, S, B, or I without knowing much about them? One of the ways is by listening to their words.

One of my rich dad's greatest skills was being able to "read" people, but he also believed you could not judge a book by its cover. Rich dad, like Henry Ford, didn't have an excellent education, but both men knew how to hire and work with people who did. Rich dad always explained to me that the ability to bring smart people together and work as a team was one of his primary skills.

When I was nine, my rich dad began to teach me the skills necessary to be successful in the B and I quadrants. One of those skills was to get beyond the surface of a person and gaze into their core. Rich dad used to say, "If I listen to a person's words, I begin to see and feel their souls."

So as a young boy, I began to sit in with my rich dad when he hired people. From these interviews I learned to listen, not so much for words, but for core values—values that my rich dad said came from their souls.

E-Quadrant Words

A person who comes from the E (employee) quadrant might say: "I am looking for a safe, secure job with good pay and excellent benefits."

S-Quadrant Words

A person who comes from the S (self-employed) quadrant might say: "My rate is $75 per hour." Or "My normal commission rate is six percent of the total price." Or "I can't seem to find people who want to work and do the job right." Or "I've got more than 20 hours into this project."

B-Quadrant Words

A person operating out of the B (business-owner) quadrant might say: "I'm looking for a new president to run my company."

I-Quadrant Words

Someone operating out of the I (investor) quadrant might say: "Is my cash flow based on an internal rate of return or net rate of return?"

Words Are Tools

Once my rich dad knew who the person he was interviewing was at their core, at least for that moment, he would know what they were really looking for, what he had to offer, and what words to use when speaking to them. Rich dad always said, "Words are powerful tools."

Rich dad constantly reminded his son Mike and me of this. "If you want to be a leader of people, then you need to be a master of words."

So one of the skills necessary to be a great B is to be a master of words, knowing which words work on which kinds of people. He trained us to first listen carefully to the words a person used. Then we would know which words we should use and when to use them, in order to respond to that person in the most effective way.

Rich dad explained, "One word may excite one type of person while that same word would completely turn off another person."

For example, the word "risk" might be exciting to a person in the I quadrant, but evoke total fear to someone in the E quadrant.

To be great leaders, rich dad stressed that we first had to be great listeners. If you don't listen to the words a person uses, you'll never be able to feel their soul. And if you don't listen to their soul, you'll never know to whom you are talking.

Core Differences

The reason he would say, "Hear their words; feel their souls," is because behind the words a person chooses are the core values and core differences of that individual.

The following are some of the generalities that separate people in one quadrant from those in another:

1. *The E (Employee)*

   When I hear the words "secure" or "benefits," I get a sense of who the speaker might be at the core. The word "secure" is a word often used in response to the emotion of fear.

   If a person feels fear, then the need for security is often a commonly used phrase for someone who comes predominantly from the E quadrant. When it comes to money and jobs, there are many people who simply hate the feeling of fear that comes with economic uncertainty: hence, the desire for security. The word "benefit" means people would also like some kind of additional reward that is spelled out, a defined and assured extra compensation, such as health insurance or a retirement plan.

The key is that they want to feel secure and see it in writing. Uncertainty doesn't make them happy; certainty does. Their internal workings say, "I'll give you this if you promise to give me that in return."

They want their fear reduced by the presence of some degree of certainty, so they seek security and strong agreements when it comes to employment. They're accurate when they say, "I'm not that interested in money." For them, the idea of security is often more important than money.

Employees can be presidents of companies or janitors. It's not so much what they do, but the contractual agreement they have with the person or organization that hires them.

2. *The S (Self-employed)*
These are people who want to "be their own boss" or like to "do their own thing." I call this group the "do-it-yourselfers."

Often, when it comes to the subject of money, a hard-core S doesn't like to have his or her income dependent on other people. In other words, if S's work hard, they expect to get paid for their work.

S's don't like having the amount of money they earn dictated by someone else or by a group of people who might not work as hard as they do. If they work hard, they expect to be paid well.

Conversely, they also understand that if they don't work hard, then they don't deserve to be paid much. When it comes to money, they have fiercely independent souls.

The Emotion of Fear

So while the E often responds to the fear of not having money by seeking security, the S often responds differently. The people in this quadrant respond to fear, not by seeking security, but by taking control of the situation and doing it on their own. That is why I call the S group the do-it-yourself group. When it comes to fear and financial risk, they want to take the bull by the horns.

In this group you find well-educated professionals who spend years in school, such as doctors, lawyers, and dentists. Also in the S group are people who took educational paths other than, or in addition to, traditional school. In this group are direct-commission salespeople and real estate agents as well as small business owners like retail shopkeepers, cleaners, restaurateurs, consultants, therapists, travel agents, car mechanics, plumbers, carpenters, preachers, electricians, hair stylists, and artists.

This group's favorite song would be either "Nobody Does It Better" or "I Did It My Way."

Self-employed people are often hard-core perfectionists. They often want to do something exceptionally well. In their mind, they don't think anyone else does it better than they do, so they really don't trust anyone else to do it. In many respects, they are true artists with their own style and methods of doing things.

And that is why we hire them. If you hire a brain surgeon, you want that brain surgeon to have had years of training and experience, but most importantly, you want this brain surgeon to be a perfectionist. The same goes for a dentist, hairstylist, marketing consultant, plumber, electrician, lawyer or a corporate trainer. You, as the client hiring this person, want someone who is the best.

For people in this group, money isn't the most important thing about their work. Their independence, the freedom to do things their way, and being respected as experts in their field are much more important than mere money. When hiring them, it's best to tell them what you want done and then leave them alone to do it. They don't need or want supervision. If you meddle too much, they'll simply walk off the job and tell you to hire someone else. Remember, independence trumps money for this group.

They often have a hard time hiring other people to do what they do simply because, in their mind, nobody else is up to the task. Also, if this group trains someone to do what they do, that newly trained person often ends up leaving to "do their own thing," to "be their own boss," to "do things their way," or to "have a chance to express their individuality."

Many S types are hesitant to hire and train other people because, once trained, they often end up as their competition. This, in turn, keeps the S types working harder at doing things on their own.

3. The B (Business owner)

This group of people could almost be the opposite of the S. Those who are true B's like to surround themselves with smart people from all four categories: E, S, B, and I. Unlike the S, who doesn't like to delegate work (because no one can do it better), the B likes to delegate. The true motto of a B is, "Why do it yourself when you can hire someone to do it for you, and they can do it better?"

Henry Ford fit this mold. As one popular story goes, a group of so-called intellectuals came by to condemn Ford for being ignorant. They claimed he really didn't know much. So Ford invited them into his office and challenged them to ask him any question, and he would answer it. So this panel assembled around America's most powerful industrialist and began to ask him questions. Ford listened to their questions and, when they were through, he simply reached for several phones on his desk and called in some of his bright assistants and asked them to give the panel the answers they sought.

He ended by informing the panel that he'd rather hire smart people who went to school to come up with answers so he could leave his mind clear to do more important tasks, tasks like thinking.

One of the quotes credited to Ford goes: "Thinking is the hardest work there is. That is why so few people engage in it."

Leadership Is Bringing Out the Best in People

My rich dad's idol was Henry Ford. He had me read books about people like Ford and John D. Rockefeller, the founder of Standard Oil. Rich dad constantly encouraged Mike and me to learn the essence of leadership and the technical skills of business. In retrospect, I understand now that many people may have one or the other, but to be a successful B, you really do need to have both. I also now realize that both skills can be learned. There is a science, as well as an art, to business and leadership. For me, both are lifelong studies.

When I was a boy, my rich dad gave me the children's book *Stone Soup,* written in 1947 by Marcia Brown and still available today. He had me read this book to begin my training as a leader in business.

"Leadership," rich dad said, "is the ability to bring out the best in people." So he trained his son and me in the technical skills necessary for becoming successful in business—technical skills such as reading financial statements, marketing, sales, accounting, management, production, and negotiation. Throughout each lesson, he stressed that we needed to learn to work with and lead people. Rich dad always said, "The technical skills of business are easy. The hard part is working with people." As a reminder, I still read *Stone Soup* today because I personally have a tendency to be a tyrant, instead of a leader, when things don't go my way.

Entrepreneurial Development

I often hear the words, "I'm going to start my own business." Many people tend to believe that the way to financial security and happiness is to do your own thing or to develop a new product no one else has. So they rush out and start their own business. In many cases, this is the path they take:

Many wind up starting an S type of business and not a B type of business. Again, one is not necessarily better than the other. Both have different strengths, weaknesses, risks, and rewards. But many people who want to start a B type of business wind up with an S type of business and become stalled in their quest to move to the right side.

Many new entrepreneurs want to do this:

But they wind up instead doing this and getting stuck there:

Many then attempt to do this:

But only a few who attempt this actually make it. Why? Because the technical skills and human skills to be successful in each quadrant are different. You must learn the skills and mindset required by a quadrant in order to find true success there.

The Difference Between an S Type of Business and a B Type of Business

Those who are true B's can leave their business for a year or more and return to find their business more profitable and running better than when they left it. In a true S type of business, if the S left for a year or more, chances are there would be no business left to return to.

So what causes the difference? Saying it simply, an S owns a job; a B owns a system and then hires competent people to operate the system. Or put another way, in many cases, the S is the system. That is why they can't leave.

For example, let's take a look at a typical dentist. A dentist spends years in school learning to become a self-contained system. You, the client, get a toothache. You go see your dentist. He fixes your tooth. You pay and go home. You're happy and you tell all of your friends about your great dentist. In most cases, the dentist can do the entire job by himself. The problem is that if the dentist goes on vacation, so does his income.

B business owners can go on vacation forever because they own a system, not a job. If the B is on vacation, the money still comes in.

To be successful as a B requires:

1. Ownership or control of systems, and

2. The ability to lead people.

For S's to evolve into B's they need to convert who they are and what they know into a system, and many aren't able to do that. Or they're often too attached to the system to let go and let other people in.

Can You Make a Better Hamburger Than McDonald's?

Many people come to me for advice on how to start a company or how to raise money for a new product or idea.

I listen, usually for about 10 minutes, and within that time I can tell where their focus is. Is it the product or the business system? In those 10 minutes, I most often hear words such as these: (Remember the importance of being a good listener and allowing words to direct you to the core values of a person's soul.)

- "This is a far better product than company XYZ makes."

- "I've looked everywhere, and nobody has this product."

- "I'll give you the idea for this product; all I want is 25 percent of the profits."

- "I've been working on this (product, book, music score, invention) for years."

These are the words of a person generally operating from the left side, the E-S side.

It's important to be gentle at this time because I'm dealing with core values and ideas that have been entrenched for years, maybe handed down for generations. If I'm not gentle or patient, I could damage a fragile and sensitive launch of an idea and, more importantly, a human being ready to evolve into another quadrant.

The Hamburger and the Business

Since I need to be gentle, at this point in the conversation, I often use the "McDonald's hamburger" example for clarification. After listening to their pitch, I slowly ask, "Can you personally make a better hamburger than McDonald's?"

So far, 100 percent of the people I've talked with about their new idea or product have said yes. They can all prepare, cook and serve a better quality hamburger than McDonald's.

Next I ask them, "Can you personally build a better business system than McDonald's?"

Some people see the difference immediately, and some don't. And I would say the difference is whether the person is fixated on the left side of the quadrant, which is focused on the idea of the better burger, or on the right side of the quadrant, which is focused on the business system.

I do my best to explain that there are a lot of entrepreneurs out there offering far superior products or services than are offered by the mega-rich multinational corporations, just as there are billions of people who can make a better burger than McDonald's. But only McDonald's has created the system that has served billions of burgers.

See the Other Side

If people can begin to see this truth, I then suggest they go to McDonald's, buy a burger, and sit and look at the system that delivered that burger. Take note of the trucks that delivered the raw burger, the rancher that raised the beef, the buyer who bought the beef and the TV ads that helped sell the beef. Notice the training of young inexperienced people to say the same words, "Hello, welcome to McDonald's," as well as the decor of the franchise, the regional offices, the bakeries that bake the buns and the millions of pounds of French fries that taste exactly the same all over the world. Then include the stockbrokers raising money for McDonald's on Wall

Street. If they can begin to understand the whole picture, then they have a chance at moving to the B-I side.

The reality is that there are unlimited new ideas, billions of people with services or products to offer, millions of products, and only a few people who know how to build excellent business systems.

Bill Gates didn't build a great product. He bought somebody else's product and built a powerful global system around it.

4. **The I (Investor)**
   Investors make money with money. They don't have to work because their money is working for them.

   The I quadrant is the playground of the rich. Regardless of which quadrant people make their money in, if they hope someday to be rich, they ultimately must come to the I quadrant. It's in the I quadrant that money becomes converted to wealth.

The CASHFLOW Quadrant

The CASHFLOW Quadrant simply makes distinctions on how income is generated, whether as an E (Employee), S (Self-employed), B (Business owner) or I (Investor). The differences are summarized below.

OPT and OPM

Most of us have heard that the secrets to great riches and wealth are:

- OPT—Other People's Time
- OPM—Other People's Money

OPT and OPM are found in the B and I quadrants. For the most part, people who work in the E and S quadrants are the OP (Other People) whose time and money are being used.

A primary reason Kim and I took time to build a B type of business, rather than an S type, was because we recognized the long-term benefit of using other people's time. One of the drawbacks to being a successful S is that success simply means more hard work. In other words, good work results in more hard work and longer hours.

In designing a B type of business, success simply means increasing the system and hiring more people. In other words, you work less, earn more and enjoy more free time. The remainder of this book goes through the skills and mindset required for the right side of the CASHFLOW Quadrant. It's my experience that being successful on the right side requires a different mindset and different technical skills. If people are flexible enough to make these changes, I think they'll find the process of achieving greater financial security or freedom easy. For other people, the process might be too difficult because many people are frozen in one quadrant and one mindset.

At a minimum, you'll find out why some people work less, earn more, pay less in taxes and feel more financially secure than others. It's simply a matter of knowing which quadrant to work out of and when.

A Guide to Freedom

The CASHFLOW Quadrant is not a set of rules. It's only a guide for those who wish to use it. It guided Kim and me from financial struggle, to financial security, and then to financial freedom.

The Difference Between the Rich and Everyone Else

A few years ago, I read an article that said most rich people receive 70 percent of their income from investments, or the I quadrant, and less than 30 percent from wages, or the E quadrant. If they were an E, chances are that they were employees of their own corporation. Their income looked like this:

For most everyone else, the poor and the middle class, at least 80 percent of their income comes from wages from the E or S quadrants, and less than 20 percent from investments in the I quadrant.

The Difference Between Being Rich and Being Wealthy

In chapter one, I wrote that Kim and I were millionaires by 1989, but we weren't financially free until 1994. There's a difference between being rich and being wealthy. By 1989, our business was making us a lot of money. We were earning more and working less because the business system was growing without any more physical effort on our part. We had achieved what most people would consider financial success.

However, we still needed to convert the cash flow coming from the business into even more tangible assets that would generate additional cash flow. We had grown our business into a success. Now it was time to focus on growing our assets to the point where the cash flow from all of our assets would be greater than our living expenses.

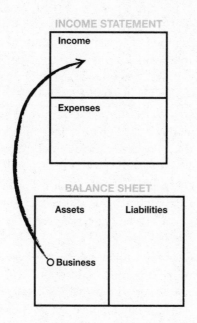

By 1994, the passive income from all of our assets was greater than our expenses. At that point, we were wealthy.

Our business is considered an asset because it generated income and operated without much physical input. For our own personal sense of wealth, we wanted to make sure we also had tangible assets, such as real estate and stocks, that were throwing off more passive income than our expenses before we claimed to be wealthy. Once the income coming from tangible assets in our asset column was greater than the money coming in from the business, we sold the business to our partner. We were now wealthy.

The Definition of Wealth

The definition of wealth is the number of days you can survive without physically working (or anyone else in your household physically working) and still maintain your standard of living.

For example, if your monthly expenses are $5,000 a month and you have $20,000 in savings, your wealth is approximately four months or 120 days. Wealth is measured in time, not dollars.

By 1994, Kim and I were wealthy indefinitely (barring great economic changes) because the income from our investments was greater than our monthly expenses.

Ultimately, it's not how much money you make that matters, but how much money you keep, and how long that money works for you. Every day I meet many people who make a lot of money, but all of their money goes out the expense column.

Every time they make a little more money, they go shopping. They often buy a bigger house or new car which results in long-term debt and more hard work. Nothing is left to go into the asset column. The money goes out so fast that you'd think they took some kind of financial laxative.

Their cash-flow pattern looks like this:

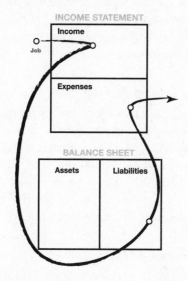

Red-Line Finances

In the world of cars, there's a saying about "keeping the engine at red line." "Red line" means the throttle is keeping the RPMs of the engine close to the red line, the maximum speed the car's engine can maintain without blowing up.

Many people, rich and poor, operate constantly at the financial red line of their personal finances. No matter how much money they make, they spend it as fast as it comes in. The trouble with operating your car's engine at red line is that the life expectancy of the engine is shortened. The same is true with operating your finances at the red line.

Several of my doctor friends say that one of the main problems they see today is stress caused by working hard and never having enough money. One says that the biggest cause of health disorders is something she calls "cancer of the wallet."

Money Making Money

Regardless of how much money people make, ultimately they should put some in the I quadrant. The I quadrant is where your money makes more money. It's based on the idea that your money works hard so you don't have to work. Although the I quadrant is important to your financial health, there are other forms of investing worth noting.

Other Forms of Investing

People invest in their education. Traditional education is important. The more education you have, the better your chances may be to earn more money, depending on your choice of profession. Given that the average person spends 40 years or more actively working, college or some type of higher education may be a good investment.

Giving your loyalty and best efforts to an employer is another form of investment. In return, via contract, the employee is rewarded with a pension for life. This was a form of investment popular in the Industrial Age that is now almost obsolete in the Information Age.

Other people invest in having large families and, in turn, have their children care for them in their old age. That form of investing was the norm in the past, yet due to economic constraints in the present, it has become more difficult for families to handle the living and medical expenses of parents.

Government retirement programs such as Social Security and Medicare, which are often paid for through payroll deductions, are another form of investment mandated by law. Due to massive changes in demographics and costs, this form of investment will probably not be able to keep many of the promises it has made.

And there are independent investment vehicles for retirement that are called individual retirement plans. Often, the federal government will offer tax incentives to both the employer and employee to participate in such plans. In America, one popular plan is the 401(k) retirement plan. In countries such as Australia, they are called superannuation plans.

Income Received from Investments

Although the above are all forms of investing, the I quadrant focuses on investments that generate income on an ongoing basis during your working years. So to qualify as a person who operates as an I, use the same criteria used in all the other quadrants. Do you receive current income from the I quadrant? In other words, is your money working for you and generating current income for you?

Let's look at a person who buys a house as an investment and rents it out. If the rent collected is greater than the expenses to operate the property, that income is coming from the I quadrant. The same is true for people who receive interest from savings, or dividends from stocks and bonds. So the qualifier for the I quadrant is how much income you generate from the quadrant without working in it.

Is My Retirement Account a Form of Investment?

Regularly putting money into a retirement account is the form of investing people in the E quadrant are most encouraged to take. These retirement plans are not without risk and, even when they perform, the rate of return is never going to make you financially free. Most of us want to be investors when our working years are over, but for the sake of this book, the I quadrant represents a person whose income comes from investments during their working years. In reality, most people aren't investing in a retirement account. Instead, most are saving money in their retirement account, hoping that when they retire, there will be more money coming out than they put in.

There's a difference between people who save money in their retirement accounts and people who, through investing, actively use their money to make more money as income.

Are Stockbrokers Investors?

Many financial advisors in the investment world are, by definition, not really people who generate their income from the I quadrant.

For example, most stockbrokers, real estate agents, financial advisors, bankers, and accountants are predominantly E's or S's. In other words, their income comes from their professional work, not necessarily from assets they own.

I have friends who are stock traders. They buy stocks low and hope to sell high. In reality, their profession is trading, much like a person who owns a retail shop and buys items at wholesale and sells them at retail. There's still something they physically must do to generate the money, so they would fit more into the S quadrant than the I quadrant.

Can all of these people be investors? The answer is yes, but it is important to know the difference between someone who earns money from commissions, sells advice by the hour, or tries to buy low and sell high compared to someone who earns money from spotting or creating good investments.

There's one way to find out how good your advisors are: Ask them what percentage of their income comes from commissions or fees versus the percentage that comes from passive income from their investments or other businesses they own.

I have several CPA friends who tell me, without violating client confidentiality, that many professional investment advisors have little in the way of income from investments. In other words, "They don't practice what they preach."

Advantages of Income from the I Quadrant

So the primary distinction of people who earn their money from the I quadrant is that they focus on having their money make money. If they're good at it, they can have that money work for them and for their family for hundreds of years.

Besides the obvious advantages of knowing how to make money with money and not having to get up and go to work, there are also many tax advantages that aren't available to people who have to work for their money.

One of the reasons the rich get richer is because they can make millions and pay, legally, little or no tax on that money. That's because they make money in the asset column, not in the income column. They make money as investors, not workers.

Moreover, people who work for money are often taxed at higher rates than investors, and their taxes are withheld from their wages. They never even see that portion of their income.

Why Aren't More People Investors?

The I quadrant is the quadrant for working less, earning more, and paying less in taxes. So why aren't more people investors? The reason is the same reason many people don't start their own businesses. It can be summed up in one word: risk.

Many people don't like the idea of handing over their hard-earned money and, possibly, not having it come back. Many people are so afraid of losing that they choose not to invest, no matter how much money they could make in return.

A Hollywood celebrity once said: "It's not return on the investment that I worry about. It's the return of the investment."

This fear of losing money seems to divide investors into four broad categories:

1. People who are risk-averse and do nothing but play it safe, keeping their money in the bank

2. People who turn the job of investing over to someone else, such as a financial advisor or a mutual-fund manager

3. Gamblers

4. Investors

The difference between a gambler and an investor is simple. For a gambler, investing is a game of chance. For an investor, investing is a game of skill. And for the people who turn their money over to someone else to invest, investing is often a game they don't want to learn. The important thing for these individuals is to choose a financial advisor carefully.

Later in this book, I'll go into the five levels of investors which should shed more light on this subject.

Risk Can Be Virtually Eliminated

The good news about investing is that risk can be greatly minimized or even eliminated, and you can still receive high yields on your money, if you know the game.

A true investor wants to recoup his or her money quickly. People who have a retirement account have to wait years to find out if they'll ever get their money back. This is the most extreme difference between a professional investor and someone who sets money aside for retirement.

It's the fear of losing money that causes most people to seek security. Yet the I quadrant is not as treacherous as many people think. The I quadrant is like any other quadrant. It has its own skills and mindset. The skills to be successful in the I quadrant can be learned if you're willing to take the time to learn.

A New Age Begins

In 1989 the Berlin Wall was torn down, as was communism. This, in my opinion, signaled the end of the Industrial Age and the start of the Information Age.

The Difference Between Industrial-Age Pension Plans and Information-Age Pension Plans

The voyage of Columbus in 1492 roughly coincides with the start of the Industrial Age. The fall of the Berlin Wall in 1989 is the event that marked the end of that age. For some reason, it seems that every 500 years in modern history, great cataclysmic changes occur. We're in one such period right now.

That change has already threatened the financial security of hundreds of millions of people, most of whom are not yet aware of the financial impact of that change and many of whom can't afford it. The change is found in the difference between an Industrial-Age pension plan and an Information-Age pension plan.

When I was a boy, my rich dad encouraged me to take risks with my money and learn to invest. He'd always say, "If you want to get rich, you need to learn how to take risks. Learn to be an investor."

At home I told my educated dad about my rich dad's suggestion that we learn how to invest and manage risk. My educated dad replied, "I don't need to learn how to invest. I have a government pension plan, a pension from the teachers union, and guaranteed Social Security benefits. Why take risks with my money?"

My educated dad believed in Industrial-Age pension plans, such as government-employee pensions and Social Security. He was happy when I signed up for the U.S. Marine Corps. Instead of being worried that I might lose my life in Vietnam, he simply said, "Stay in for 20 years, and you'll get a pension and medical benefits for life."

Although still in use, such pension plans are becoming obsolete. The idea of a company being financially responsible for your retirement and the government picking up the balance of your retirement needs through pension schemes is an old, outdated idea.

People Need to Become Investors

As we move from defined-benefit pension plans (or what I call Industrial-Age retirement plans) to defined-contribution pension plans (or Information-Age pension plans), the result is that you, as an individual, must now be financially responsible for yourself. Amazingly, few people have noticed the change and understand its ramifications.

Industrial-Age Pension Plans

In the Industrial Age, a defined-benefit pension plan meant that the company guaranteed you, the worker, a defined amount of money (usually paid monthly) for as long as you lived. People felt secure because these plans assured a steady income.

Information-Age Pension Plans

But in 1974, the rules changed with the passage of the Employee Retirement Income Security Act (ERISA). Suddenly, companies were no longer guaranteeing financial security at the end of your working days. Instead, employers began offering defined-contribution retirement plans. "Defined contribution" means that you only get back what you and the company have contributed while you were working. In other words, your pension is defined solely by what has been contributed. If you and your company put no money in, then you get no money out.

The good news is that, in the Information Age, life expectancy has increased. The bad news is that you might outlive your pension (if you even have one).

Risky Pension Plans

What many people don't understand is that whatever you and your employer put into the plan is no longer guaranteed to exist when you decide to pull it out. This is because plans like the 401(k) and the superannuation are subject to market forces. In other words, one day you could have a million dollars in the account. But, if there were a stock-market crash, which every market occasionally has, your million dollars could be cut in half or even wiped out. With defined-contribution plans, the guarantee of lifelong income is gone.

People today, who retire at age 65 and begin to live on their defined-contribution plan, could run out of money by, let's say, age 75. Then what do they do? Dust off the resumé?

And what about the government's defined-benefit pension plan? Well, in the United States, Social Security is expected to be bankrupt by the year 2037, with Medicare bankrupt by 2017. Even today, Social Security doesn't provide much in the way of income. What will happen when 77 million baby boomers begin to want the money they paid in, but it's not there?

In 1998, President Clinton's popular cry of "Save Social Security" was well received. Yet as Democratic Senator Ernest Hollings pointed out, "Obviously, the first way to save Social Security is to stop looting it." For decades, the federal government has been responsible for "borrowing" the retirement money for expenditures: a government-sanctioned Ponzi scheme.

Many politicians seem to think that Social Security is income that can be spent, rather than an asset that should be held in trust.

Too Many People Counting on the Government

I write my books and create products, such as the educational *CASHFLOW* board game, because the Industrial Age is history, and we must prepare for the opportunities of the Information Age.

My concern as a private citizen is that, from my generation forward, we aren't properly prepared to handle the differences between the Industrial Age and the Information Age. A case in point is how we prepare financially for our retirement years. The idea of "go to school and get a safe, secure job" was a good one for people born before 1930. Today, everyone needs to go to school to prepare for a job or career, but we also need to know how to invest—and investing is not a subject taught in school.

One of the problems created by the Industrial Age is that too many people are dependent upon the government to solve their individual problems. Today we're facing even bigger problems because we have delegated our personal financial responsibility to the government.

It's estimated that by the year 2020, there will be 275 million Americans, with 100 million of them expecting some kind of government support. This will include federal employees, military retirees, postal workers, teachers, other government employees, and retirees expecting Social Security and Medicare payments. They're contractually correct in expecting government support because, in one way or another, most have been investing into that promise throughout their working lives. Unfortunately, there were too many promises made for too many years. Now the bill is coming due.

I don't think those financial promises can be kept. If our government begins to raise taxes even higher to pay for those promises, those who can escape will escape to countries that have lower taxes. In the Information Age, the term "offshore" won't necessarily mean another country as a tax haven. Offshore could mean cyberspace.

A Great Change Is at Hand

I recall President John F. Kennedy warning, "A great change is at hand." Well, that change is here.

Investing without Being Investors

The change from defined-benefit to defined-contribution pension plans is forcing millions of people throughout the world to become investors, with little investor education. Many people who have spent their lives avoiding financial risks are now being forced to take them. Most will find out when it comes time to retire whether they were wise investors, or careless gamblers.

Today, the stock market is fueled by many things, one of which is non-investors trying to become investors.

Their financial path looks like this:

A large majority of these people, the E's and S's, are people who by nature are security-oriented. That's why they seek secure jobs or start small businesses they can control. Because of the defined-contribution retirement plans, they're migrating today to the I quadrant where they hope they'll find security when their working years are over. Unfortunately, the I quadrant is not known for its security. The I quadrant is the quadrant of risk.

Because so many people on the left side of the CASHFLOW Quadrant come looking for security, the stock market responds in kind.

That's why you often hear the following words:

1. *Diversification*

People who seek security use the word "diversification" a lot. Why? Because the strategy of diversification is an investment strategy for "not losing." It's not an investment strategy for winning. Successful or rich investors don't diversify. They focus their efforts.

Warren Buffett, possibly the world's greatest investor, says this about diversification: "The strategy we've adopted precludes our following standard diversification dogma. Many pundits would therefore say the strategy must be riskier than that employed by more conventional investors. We disagree. We believe that a policy of portfolio concentration may well decrease risk if it raises, as it should, both the intensity with which an investor thinks about a business and the comfort level he must feel with its economic characteristics before buying into it."

In other words, Warren Buffett is saying that portfolio concentration, or focusing on a few investments rather than diversifying, is a better strategy. In his mind, concentration rather than diversification requires you to become smarter and more intense in your thoughts and actions. His article goes on to say that average investors avoid volatility because they think volatility is risky. Warren Buffet says instead, "In fact, the true investor welcomes volatility."

When Kim and I were escaping from financial struggle to financial freedom, we didn't diversify. We concentrated our investments.

2. **Blue chip stocks**
Security-minded investors usually buy blue-chip companies. Why? Because in their mind, they're safer. While the company might be safer, the stock market is not. These stocks won't protect your money in a market free fall.

3. **Mutual funds**
People who know little about investing feel more secure turning their money over to a fund manager who they hope will do a better job than they can. This is a smart strategy for people who have no intention of becoming professional investors. But the problem is that, as smart as this strategy is, it doesn't mean that mutual funds are less risky.

Today, the market is filled with millions of people who, by nature, are security-minded. But, due to the changing economy, they are being forced to cross from the left side of the CASHFLOW Quadrant into the right side, where their brand of security doesn't really exist. That causes me concern.

Great Economic Upheavals Coming

The stage is set for a great economic upheaval. Such upheavals have always marked the end of an old era and the birth of a new one. At the end of every age, there are people who move forward, and other people who cling to ideas of the past. I'm afraid that people who still believe their financial security is the responsibility of a big company or big government will be disappointed in the coming years. Those are ideas of the Industrial Age, not the Information Age.

No one has a crystal ball. I subscribe to many investment news services and each one says something different. Some say the near future is bright. Some say a market crash and major depression are right around the corner. To remain objective, I listen to both sides, because both have points worth listening to. I do not play fortune-teller, trying to predict the future. Instead, I work at staying educated in both the B and I quadrants and being prepared for whatever happens. A person who is prepared will prosper no matter which direction the economy goes, whenever it goes.

If history is any indicator, a person who lives to the age of 75 should anticipate going through one depression and two major recessions during his or her lifetime. My parents went through their depression, but the baby boomers have not—yet.

Today we all need to be concerned with more than just job security. I think we must also focus on our own long-term financial security and not leave that responsibility to a company or the government. The times officially changed when companies said that they were no longer responsible for your retirement years. Once they switched to the defined-contribution retirement plan, the message was that you were now responsible for investing in your own retirement. Today, we all need to become wiser investors, always aware of the ups and downs of the financial markets.

I recommend learning to be an investor rather than giving your money to somebody else to invest for you. If you simply turn your money over to a mutual fund or to an advisor, you may have to wait until you're 65 tofind out if that person did a good job. If they did a lousy job, you may have to work for the rest of your life. Millions of people will have to do just that because it will be too late for them to invest or learn about investing.

Learn to Manage Risk

It is possible to invest for high returns with low risk. All you have to do is learn how it's done. It is not hard. In fact, it's much like learning how to ride a bike. In the early stages, you may fall down, but after a while, the falling stops and investing becomes second nature, just as riding a bicycle is for most of us.

The problem with the left side of the CASHFLOW Quadrant is that most people go there to avoid financial risk. Instead of avoiding risk, I recommend learning how to manage financial risk.

Take a Risk

People who take risks change the world. Few people ever get rich without taking risks. Too many people have come to depend on government to eliminate the risks of life. The beginning of the Information Age should have ushered in an era of smaller government because big government is frankly too expensive to maintain. But rather than becoming savvy, educated investors, millions of people around the world have bought into the archaic idea of entitlements and pensions for life. This simply isn't feasible. The Information Age means we all need to become more self-sufficient, grow up and take personal responsibility for our retirement.

The idea of "study hard and find a safe, secure job" is an idea born in the Industrial Age. We're not in that age anymore. The times are changing. The problem is that many people's ideas have not changed. They still think they're entitled to something. Many still think that the I quadrant is not their responsibility. They continue to think that the government, big business, a labor union, their mutual funds, or their family will take care of them when their working days are over. For their sake, I hope they're right. These individuals have no need to read further.

Rich Dad's CASHFLOW Quadrant was written to help individuals who want to make the move from the left side to the right side but don't know where to start. Anyone can make the move with the right skills and determination.

If you've already found your own financial freedom, I say, "Congratulations." Please tell others about your path and guide them if they want to be guided. Teach them, but let them find their own path, for there are many paths to financial freedom.

Regardless of what you decide, please remember this: Financial freedom might be free, but it doesn't come cheap. Freedom has a price, and to me it's worth that price. The big secret is this: It takes neither money to be financially free, nor a good formal education. It also doesn't have to be risky. Instead, freedom's price is measured in dreams, desire, and the ability to overcome disappointments that occur along the way. Are you willing to pay the price?

One of my fathers paid the price. The other didn't. But he paid a different kind of price.

The B-Quadrant Quiz

Are you a true business owner?

You are if you can answer "Yes" to the following question:

Can you leave your business for a year or more and return to find it more profitable and running better than when you left it?

◯ Yes
◯ No

Chapter Three
WHY PEOPLE CHOOSE SECURITY OVER FREEDOM

---

*Many people seek job security because
that's what they are taught, both at school and at home.*

Both of my dads recommended that I go to college and get a degree. But it was after receiving the degree that their advice took different paths. My highly educated dad constantly advised: "Go to school, get good grades, and then get a good safe, secure job."

He was recommending a life path focused on the left side of the CASHFLOW Quadrant that looks like this:

Their advice was different because one dad was concerned with job security, and the other focused on financial freedom.

Why People Seek Job Security

The primary reason many people seek job security is because that's what they are taught to seek, both at school and at home.

As adults, millions of people still continue to follow that advice. Many of us are conditioned from our earliest days to think about job security, rather than financial security or financial freedom. And because most of us learn little to nothing about money at home or at school, it's only natural that we cling ever more tightly to the idea of job security instead of reaching for freedom.

If you look at the CASHFLOW Quadrant, you'll notice that the left side is motivated by security. The right side is motivated by freedom.

Trapped by Debt

The main reason that 90 percent of the population is working on the left side is because that's the side they learned about at school. After leaving school, they often end up with lots of expenses and may fall into debt. This means they must cling ever tighter to a job, or to professional security, just to pay the bills.

I often meet young people who receive their college diploma along with the bill for their college loans. Several of them told me that they're depressed when they see that they are in debt thousands and thousands of dollars for their college education. If their parents paid the bill, then the parents are strapped financially for years.

Most Americans today will receive a credit card while still in school and will be in debt for the rest of their lives. That's because they're often following a script that became popular in the Industrial Age.

Following the Script

If we track the life of an average educated person, the financial script often goes like this:

The child goes to school, graduates, finds a job, and soon has some money to spend. The young adult now can afford to rent an apartment, buy electronics, new clothes, some furniture, and, of course, a car. Soon the bills begin to come in.

One day, the adult meets someone special and sparks fly. They fall in love and get married. For a while, life is blissful because two can live as cheaply as one. With only one rent to pay, they can afford to set a few dollars aside to buy the dream of all young couples—their own home.

They find a house, pull their money out of savings and use it for a down payment. Now they have a mortgage. Because they have a new house, they need new furnishings, so they find a furniture store that advertises those magic words: "No money down. Easy monthly payments."

Life is wonderful, and they throw a party to have all their friends over to see their new house, new car, new furniture, and new toys. They're already deeply in debt. Then the first child arrives.

After dropping the child off at nursery school, this average couple must now put their nose to the grindstone and go to work. They become trapped by the need for job security simply because, on average, they're less than three months away from financial bankruptcy. These people will often say, "I can't afford to quit. I have bills to pay."

The Success Trap

One of the reasons I learned so much from my rich dad was because he had the free time to teach me. As he grew more successful, he had more free time and money. His business got better, but he didn't have to work harder. He simply had his president expand the system and hire more people to do the work. If his investments did well, he reinvested the money and made more money. Instead of working, he spent hours with his son and me explaining to us everything he was doing in business and investing. I was learning more from him than I was learning at school. That's what happens when you work hard on the right side of the CASHFLOW Quadrant, the B and I side.

My highly educated dad worked hard too, but he worked hard on the left side. By working hard, getting promoted, and taking on more responsibility, he had less and less free time to spend with his kids. He would leave for work at 7 a.m., and many times we wouldn't see him because we had to go to bed before he got home. That's what happens when you work hard and become successful in the E and S quadrants. Success brings you less and less time, even if it does bring more money.

The Money Trap

Success on the B and I side requires a particular kind of knowledge about money called "financial intelligence." Rich dad said that financial intelligence determined, not so much how much money you make, but how much money you keep, how hard that money works for you, and how many generations you can keep it.

Success on the right side requires financial intelligence. If people lack basic financial intelligence, they'll find it hard to survive on the right side of the CASHFLOW Quadrant.

My rich dad was good with money and with people at work. He had to be. He was responsible for creating money, managing as few people as possible, keeping costs low, and keeping profits high. Those are the skills necessary for success on the right side.

It was my rich dad who stressed that your home is not an asset, but a liability. He could prove it simply by looking at the numbers.

My educated dad didn't manage money and people at work, although he thought he did. As the state superintendent of education, he was a government official with a multimillion dollar budget and thousands of employees. But it was not money he created. It was the taxpayers' money, and his job was to spend all of it. If he didn't spend it, the government would give him less money the next year. So at the end of each fiscal year, his goal was to deplete his budget, which meant he often hired more people to justify the next year's budget. The funny thing was that the more people he hired, the more problems he had.

As a young boy observing both fathers, I began to take mental notes of what kind of life I wanted to lead.

My educated dad was a voracious reader of books, so he was word-literate, but he was not financially literate. Because he couldn't read numbers on a financial statement, he had to take the advice of his banker and accountant, and both told him that his house was an asset and that it should be his largest investment.

Because of this financial advice, not only did my highly educated dad work harder, he also got further into debt. Every time he received a promotion for his hard work, he also got a pay raise, and with each pay raise he went into a higher tax bracket. Because he was in a high tax bracket, and taxes for high-income workers in the 1960s and 1970s were extremely high, his accountant and banker would tell him to buy a bigger house so he could write off the interest payments. He made more money, but all that happened was that his taxes increased and his debt increased. The more successful he got, the harder he had to work, and the less time he had with the people he loved. Soon, all the children were gone, and he was still working hard just to keep up with the bills.

He always thought that the next promotion and pay raise would solve his problem. But the more money he made, the more the same things happened. He got deeper into debt and paid more in taxes.

The more frazzled he got, both at home and at work, the more he seemed to depend on job security. The more emotionally attached he got to his job and to a paycheck to pay the bills, the more he encouraged his kids to "get a safe, secure job."

The more insecure he felt, the more he sought security.

Your Two Biggest Expenses

Because my dad couldn't read financial statements, he failed to see the money trap he was getting sucked into as he grew more successful. It's the same money trap I see millions of other successful hardworking people fall into.

The reason so many people struggle financially is because, every time they make more money, they also increase their two biggest expenses: taxes and interest on debt.

To top it all off, the government often offers you tax breaks to get you deeper into debt. Doesn't that make you a little suspicious?

At the end of my hardworking, educated dad's life, the little money he did have left to pass on was taken by the government in probate taxes.

The Search for Freedom

I know that many people search for freedom and happiness. The problem is that most people haven't been trained to work from the B and I quadrants. They have been trained instead to search for job security. Because of this training and their increasing debt, most people limit their search for financial freedom to the left side of the CASHFLOW Quadrant. Unfortunately, financial security and financial freedom are seldom found in the E or the S quadrant. True security and freedom are only found on the right side.

Going from Job to Job in Search of Freedom

One thing the CASHFLOW Quadrant is useful for is to track or observe a person's life pattern. Many people spend their life in search of security or freedom, but wind up instead going from job to job.

For example, I have a friend from high school who I hear from about every five years. He is always excited because he has found the perfect job and the company of his dreams. He loves the company. It's doing exciting things. He loves his work, he has an important title, the pay is great, the people are great, the benefits are great, and his chances for promotion are great.

About four and a half years later, I hear from him again. Only this time he's dissatisfied. The company he works for is now corrupt and dishonest and, in his opinion, it doesn't treat its workers with respect. He hates his boss, he was passed over for a promotion, and they don't pay him enough. Six months go by, and he's happy again because he's found a new job. And the cycle starts anew.

His life path looks something like a dog chasing its tail. It looks like this:

His life pattern is going from job to job. So far, he lives well because he's smart, attractive, and personable. But the years are catching up with him, and younger people are now getting the jobs he used to get. He has a few thousand dollars in savings, nothing set aside for retirement, a house he'll never own, child-support payments, and college yet to pay for. His youngest child, 8, lives with his ex-wife, and his oldest child, 14, lives with him.

He used to always say to me, "I don't have to worry. I'm still young. I have time."

I wonder if he's saying that now.

In my opinion, he needs to make a serious effort to begin moving to either the B or the I quadrant quickly. A new attitude and a new educational process need to begin. Unless he gets lucky and wins the lottery, or finds a rich woman to marry, he's on a course of working hard for the rest of his life.

Doing Your Own Thing

Another common pattern is someone going from E to S. During periods of massive downsizing and unemployment, some people get the message. Instead of looking for another job, they decide to start their own businesses.

There's been a boom in so-called home-based businesses. Many people make the decision to start their own business, do their own thing, and be their own boss. Their career path looks like this:

Of all the life paths, this is the one I feel for the most. In my opinion, being an S can be extremely rewarding—and the most risky. I think the S quadrant is the hardest quadrant there is. The failure rates are high and, if you make it, being successful can be worse than failing. That's because, if you're successful as an S, you'll work harder than if you were in any of the other quadrants, and you'll work harder for a long time.

The reason S's work the hardest is because they typically are the proverbial "chief cook and bottle washer." They have to do, or be responsible for, all the jobs that are done by many managers and employees in a bigger company. An S just starting out often answers the phone, pays the bills, makes sales calls, tries to advertise on a small budget, handles customers, hires employees, fires employees, fills in when employees don't show up, talks to the tax man, fights off the government inspectors, and on and on.

Personally, I cringe whenever I hear someone say they're going to start their own business. I wish them well, yet I feel great concern for them. I've seen so many E's take their life savings or borrow money from friends and family to start their own business. After three or so years of struggle and hard work, the business folds and, instead of life savings, they have debt to pay off.

Nationally, nine out of 10 of these types of businesses fail in five years. Of the one that is remaining, nine out of 10 of them fail in the next five years. In other words, 99 out of 100 small businesses ultimately disappear in 10 years.

I think the reason most fail in the first five years is due to lack of experience and lack of capital. The reason the one survivor often fails in the second five years isn't due to lack of capital, but lack of energy. The hours of long, hard work finally get to the person. Many S's just burn out.

Those who do survive seem to have become used to the idea of getting up, going to work, and working hard forever. That seems to be all they know and all they do.

I have a friend whose parents have spent the last 45 years working long hours in their liquor store. As crime increased in their neighborhood, they had to put steel bars up on the doors and all the windows. Today, money is passed through a slot, much like in a bank. I go by occasionally to see them. They're wonderful, sweet people, but it saddens me to see them as virtual prisoners in their own business, from 10 in the morning until two the next morning, staring out from behind the bars.

Many wise S's sell their businesses at their peak, before they run out of steam, to someone with energy and money. They take some time off and then start something new. They keep doing their own thing and love it. The key is to know when to get out.

The Worst Advice to Give Your Children

If you were born prior to 1930, then "Go to school, get good grades, and find a safe, secure job" was good advice. But for most of you, it's bad advice.

Why? The answer is found in taxes and debt.

For people who earn their income from the E quadrant, there are virtually no tax breaks left. Today in America, being an employee means you are a 50/50 partner with the government. That means the government ultimately will take 50 percent or more of an employee's earnings, and much of that before the employee even sees the paycheck.

When you consider that the government offers you tax breaks for going further into debt, the path to financial freedom is virtually impossible for most people in the E and S quadrants. I often hear accountants tell clients who begin earning more income from the E quadrant to buy a bigger house so they can receive a bigger tax break. While that may make sense to someone on the left side of the CASHFLOW Quadrant, it makes no sense to someone on the right side.

Who Pays the Most Taxes?

The rich do not pay a lot in income taxes. Why? Simply because they don't earn their money as employees. The ultra-rich know that the best way to avoid taxes legally is by generating income out of the B and I quadrants.

If people earn money in the E quadrant, the only tax break they're offered is to buy a bigger house and go into greater debt. Viewed from the right side of the CASHFLOW Quadrant, that isn't financially intelligent. To people on the right side, that's like saying, "Give me $1, and I will give you 50 cents back."

Taxes Are Unfair

I often hear people say, "It's un-American not to pay taxes." Americans who say this seem to have forgotten their history. America was founded out of tax protest. Have they forgotten the famous Boston Tea Party of 1773? This rebellion sparked the Revolutionary War and was all about taxation—taxation without representation.

This rebellion was followed by Shays' Rebellion, the Whiskey Rebellion, Fries's Rebellion, the Tariff Wars, and many others throughout the history of the United States.

There are two other famous tax revolts that weren't staged by Americans, but do demonstrate the passion with which people object to taxation.

The story of William Tell is a story of tax protest. That's why he was forced to shoot the apple off his son's head. He was angry about taxes and refused to bow to the tax collector. His punishment was to put his son's life at risk with a target on his head.

And then there was Lady Godiva. She pleaded with her husband, the Earl of Mercia, to lower taxes in her town. Her husband said he would lower the taxes if she would ride naked through the town. She took him up on his offer.

Tax Advantages

Taxes may be a necessity of modern civilization, but problems arise when taxes become abusive and mismanaged. As millions of baby boomers begin to retire, they will shift from the role of taxpayers

to retirees and Social Security recipients. There will
be a need to collect more taxes to support this shift.
America and other great nations will decline financially.
Individuals with money will leave in search of countries
that welcome their money, instead of penalizing them
for having it.

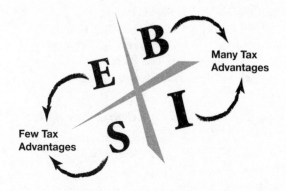

A Big Mistake

A newspaper reporter once asked me how much
money I made during the prior year. I replied,
"Approximately a million dollars."

"And how much did you pay in taxes?" he asked.

"Nothing," I said. "That money was made in
capital gains and I was able to indefinitely defer
paying those taxes. I sold three pieces of real estate
and put them through a Section 1031 exchange
under the U.S. Internal Revenue Code. I never
touched the money. I just reinvested it into a much

larger property." A few days later, the newspaper ran this story.

"Rich man makes $1 million and admits to paying nothing in taxes."

I did say something like that, but a few choice words were missing, which distorted the message. I don't know if the reporter was being malicious or if he simply didn't understand what a 1031 exchange is. Whatever the reason, it's a perfect example of different points of view coming from different quadrants. As I said, not all income is equal. Some income is much less taxed than others.

Most People Focus on Income, Not Assets

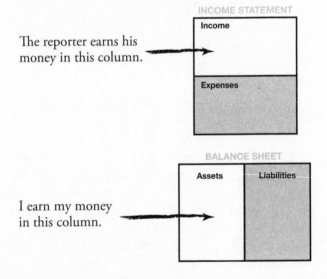

The reporter earns his money in this column.

I earn my money in this column.

The reporter earns his money in this quadrant.

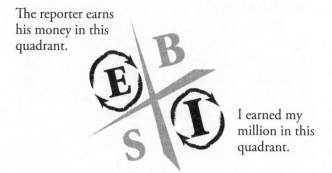

I earned my million in this quadrant.

Today, I still hear people say, "I'm going back to school so I can get a raise," or "I'm working hard so I can get a promotion."

Those are words or ideas of a person who is focusing on the income column of the financial statement or the E quadrant. Those are the words of a person who will give half of that raise to the government and work harder and longer to do it.

In an upcoming chapter, I'll explain how people on the right side of the CASHFLOW Quadrant utilize taxes as an asset, instead of the liability it is for most people on the left side. It's not a matter of being unpatriotic. It's about fighting back legally to defend the right to keep as much money as possible. Countries where people don't protest their taxes often have depressed economies.

Get Rich Quickly

For Kim and me to go from homeless to financially free quickly meant earning our money in the B and I quadrants. In these quadrants, you can get rich quickly because you can avoid paying taxes legally. And by being able to keep more money and have that money work for us, we found freedom quickly.

How to Get Free

Debt and taxes are the main reasons most people never feel financially secure or achieve financial freedom. The path to security or freedom is found on the right side of the CASHFLOW Quadrant. You need to go beyond job security and know the difference between financial security and financial freedom.

As you know, my highly educated dad was fixated on job security, as are most people of his generation. He assumed that job security meant financial security—until, that is, he lost his job and couldn't find another. My rich dad never talked about job security. He talked instead about financial freedom.

The answer to finding the kind of security or freedom you desire can be found in observing the patterns found in the CASHFLOW Quadrant.

The Pattern for Job Security

People who follow this pattern are often good at performing their job. Many spent years in school and years on the job gaining experience. The problem is that they know little about the B quadrant or the I quadrant, even if they have a retirement plan. They feel financially insecure because they've been trained only for job security.

Knowledge Is Power

To become more financially secure, I suggest that, in addition to performing their jobs in the E or S quadrants, individuals become educated in the B or I quadrants. By having confidence in their abilities on both sides of the CASHFLOW Quadrant, they'll naturally feel more secure, even if they have only a little money. Knowledge is power, and when an opportunity presents itself, they will be prepared to act with confidence.

That is why our maker gave us two legs. If we had only one leg, we would always feel wobbly and insecure. By having knowledge in two quadrants, one on the left and one on the right, we tend to feel more secure. People who know about their job or their profession only have one leg. Every time the economic winds blow, they tend to wobble more than people with two legs.

The Pattern for Financial Security

This is the pattern for financial security for an E:

Instead of just putting money into a retirement account and hoping for the best, this loop signifies that people feel confident in their education as both an investor and an employee. Just as we study at school to learn a job, I suggest you study to become a professional investor.

The reporter who was upset about my making a million dollars in my asset column and not paying taxes never asked me the question, "How did you make the million dollars?"

To me, that's the real question. Legally avoiding the taxes is easy. Making the million wasn't so easy.

A second path to financial security could be:

And this is what financial security looks like for an S:

The average American millionaire is self-employed, lives frugally, and invests for the long term. The pattern above reflects that financial life path.

This path, the S to the B, is often the path that many great entrepreneurs like Bill Gates take. It's not the easiest but, in my mind, it is one of the best.

Two Are Better Than One

Back in chapter two, I discussed how the average rich person earns 70 percent of their income from the right side and less than 30 percent from the left side. I've found that no matter how much money people make, they will feel more secure if they operate in more than one quadrant. Financial security is having a secure footing on both sides of the CASHFLOW Quadrant.

Millionaire Firefighters

I have two friends who are examples of success on both sides of the CASHFLOW Quadrant. They have tremendous job security with benefits, and they have also achieved great financial wealth on the right side. Both are firefighters who work for the city government. They enjoy good, steady pay, excellent benefits and retirement plans, and work only two days a week. Three days a week they work as professional investors. The remaining two days, they relax and spend time with their families.

One buys old houses, fixes them up, and collects rent. He owns 45 houses that pay him $10,000 a month net after debt, taxes, maintenance, and management and insurance. He earns $3,500 a month as a firefighter, making his total monthly income more than $13,000 and his annual income about $150,000 and growing. He has five more years before retirement, and his goal is to have $200,000 a year in income at age 56. Not bad for a government employee with four kids.

The other friend spends his time analyzing companies and taking major long-term positions in stocks and options. His portfolio is now more than "$3 million. If he cashed it out and moved the money into an investment that earns 10 percent interest a year, he would have an income of approximately $300,000 per year for life (even taking into account average market fluctuations). Again, not bad for a government employee with two kids.

Both friends have enough passive income from their 20 years of investing to have retired by age 40, but they both enjoy their work and want to retire with full benefits. Then they'll be free to enjoy the benefits of success gained from both sides of the CASHFLOW Quadrant.

Money Alone Does Not Bring Security

I have met many people who have millions in their retirement accounts and still feel insecure. Why? Because it's money generated from their job or business. They often have the money invested in a retirement account, but know little to nothing about the subject of investments. If that money disappears and their working days are over, what do they do then?

In times of great economic change, there are always great transfers of wealth. Even if you don't have much money, it's important to invest in your education because, when the changes come, you'll be better prepared to handle them. Don't be caught unaware and afraid. As I said, no one can predict what will happen, so it's best to be prepared for whatever happens. And that means getting educated now.

The Pattern for Financial Freedom

This is the pattern my rich dad recommended. It is the path to financial freedom. This is true financial freedom because, in the B quadrant, people are working for you, and in the I quadrant, your money is working for you. You are free to work or not to work. Your knowledge in these two quadrants has brought you complete physical freedom from work.

If you look at the ultra-rich, this is their pattern. The loop around the B and the I signifies the income pattern of people like Bill Gates, Rupert Murdoch, and Warren Buffett.

A quick word of caution: The B quadrant is much different from the I quadrant. I've seen many successful B's sell their businesses for millions, and their new-found wealth goes to their head. They tend to think that their dollars are a measure of their IQ, so they swagger on down to the I quadrant and lose it all. The game and rules are different in all of the quadrants, which is why I recommend education over an ego trip.

Just as in the case of financial security, having two quadrants gives you greater stability in the world of financial freedom.

A Choice of Paths

The preceding patterns are the different financial paths people can choose. Unfortunately, most people choose the path of job security. When the economy starts wobbling, they cling ever more desperately to job security and wind up spending their lives pursuing it.

At a minimum, I recommend becoming educated in financial security, which is feeling confident about your job and feeling confident about your ability to invest in good and bad times. A big secret is that true investors make more money in bad markets. They make their money because the non-investors are panicking and selling when they should be buying. I'm not afraid of the possible coming economic changes, because change means wealth is being transferred.

Your Boss Cannot Make You Rich

A friend of mine sold his company and, on the day of the sale, put more than $15 million into his bank account. On the other hand, his employees had to look for new jobs.

At the farewell party, which was filled with tears, there were also undercurrents of extreme anger and resentment. Although he'd paid them well for years, most were financially no better off on their last day of work than they were on their first day of work. Many people realized that the owner of the company had become rich while they spent all those years collecting their paychecks and paying bills.

The reality is that your boss's job is not to make you rich. Your boss's job is to make sure you get your paycheck. It's your job to become rich if you want to. And that job begins the moment you receive your paycheck. If you have poor money-management skills, then all the money in the world won't save you. If you budget your money wisely and learn about either the B or I quadrant, then you're on your own path to great personal fortune and, most importantly, freedom.

My rich dad used to say to his son and me that the only difference between a rich person and a poor person is what they do in their spare time.

I agree with that statement. I realize that people are busier than ever before, and free time is more and more precious. Yet I believe that if you're going to be busy anyway, be busy on both sides of the CASHFLOW Quadrant. If you do that, you'll have a better chance of eventually finding more free time and more financial freedom. When at work, work hard. But remember that what you do after work with your paycheck and your spare time will determine your future. If you work hard on the left side, you'll work hard forever. If you work hard on the right side, you have a chance of finding freedom.

The Path I Recommend

I am often asked by people in the E and S quadrants, "What would you recommend?" I recommend the same path my rich dad recommended to me—the same path that people like Ross Perot and Bill Gates took. The path looks like this:

Occasionally people reply, "But I'd rather be an investor."

To which I say, "Then go to the I quadrant. If you have plenty of money and lots of free time, go straight to the I quadrant. But if you don't have an abundance of time and money, the path my rich dad recommended is safer."

I's Invest in B's

In most cases, people do not have an abundance of time and money, so they then ask another question, "Why do you recommend the B quadrant first?"

This discussion usually takes an hour or so, but I'll just summarize my reasons in the next few lines.

1. *Experience and education*

   If you are first successful as a B, you'll have a better chance of developing into a powerful I. If you first develop a solid business sense, you can become a better investor. You'll be better able to identify other good B's. True investors invest in successful B's with stable business systems. It's risky to invest in an E or an S who doesn't know the difference between a system and a product, or who lacks excellent leadership skills.

2. *Cash flow*

   If you have a business that is up and running, you then should have the free time and the cash flow to support the ups and downs of the I quadrant.

   Many times I meet people from the E and S quadrants who are so tight on cash that they can't afford to take any kind of financial loss. One market swing and they're wiped out because they operate financially at the red line.

   The reality is that investing is capital- and knowledge-intensive. Sometimes it takes lots of capital and requires a lot of time to gain the necessary knowledge. Many successful investors have lost many times before winning. Successful people know that success is a poor teacher. Learning comes from making mistakes and, in the I quadrant, mistakes cost money. If you lack both knowledge and capital, it's financial suicide to try to become an investor.

By developing the skill of becoming a good B first, you'll also be providing the cash flow necessary to help you become a good investor. The business you develop as a B will provide the cash to support you as you gain the education to become a good investor. Once you have gained the knowledge to become a successful investor, you'll understand how I can say, "It does not always take money to make money."

Good News

The good news is that it's easier than ever before to be successful in the B quadrant because of technology. Although it's not as easy as just getting a minimum-wage job, the systems are in place now for more and more people to find financial success as B's.

Chapter Four
THE THREE KINDS OF BUSINESS SYSTEMS

---

*Your goal is to own a system
and have people work that system for you.*

In moving to the B quadrant, remember that your goal is to own a system and have people work that system for you. You can develop the business system yourself, or you can look for a system to purchase. Think of the system as the bridge that will allow you to cross safely from the left side of the CASHFLOW Quadrant to the right side. It's your bridge to financial freedom.

There are three main types of business systems commonly in use today. They are:

1. Traditional C corporations—where you develop your own system
2. Franchises—where you buy an existing system
3. Network marketing—where you buy into and become part of an existing system

Each business system has its strengths and weaknesses, yet each ultimately does the same thing. If operated properly, each system will provide a steady stream of income without much physical effort on the part of the owner once it's up and running. The problem is getting it up and running.

In 1985, when people asked Kim and me why we were homeless, we simply said, "We're building a business system."

It was a business system that was a hybrid of the traditional C corporation and a franchise. As stated before, the B quadrant requires a knowledge of both systems and people.

Our decision to develop our own system meant a lot of hard work. I'd taken this route before, and my company had failed. Although it was successful for years, it suddenly went broke in its fifth year. When success came to us, we weren't ready with an adequate system. Our system began to break down even though we had hardworking people. We felt like we were on a good-size yacht that had sprung a leak in a location we could not determine.

You May Lose Two or Three Companies

When I was in high school, my rich dad told Mike and me that he had nearly lost a company when he was in his twenties. "That was the best and worst experience of my life," he said. "As much as I hated it, I learned more by repairing it and eventually turning it into a huge success."

Knowing that I was contemplating starting my own company, rich dad said to me, "You may lose two or three companies before you build a successful one that lasts."

He was training Mike to take over his empire. But because my dad was a government employee, I wasn't going to inherit an empire. I had to build my own.

Success Is a Poor Teacher

"Success is a poor teacher," rich dad always said. "We learn the most about ourselves when we fail, so don't be afraid of failing. Failing is part of the process of success. You can't have success without failure."

Maybe it was a self-fulfilling prophecy, but in 1984, my third company went down. I had made millions and lost millions and was starting all over again when I met Kim. The reason I know she didn't marry me for my money is because I didn't have any money. When I told her what I was going to do, build company number four, she didn't back away.

"I'll build it with you," was her reply, and she was true to her word. Along with another partner, we built a business system with 11 offices worldwide that generated income regardless of whether we worked or not. Building it from nothing to 11 offices took five years of blood, sweat, and tears, but it worked. Both dads were happy for me and sincerely congratulated me.

The Hard Part

Mike often said to me, "I'll never know if I can do what you or my dad did. The system was handed to me. All I had to do was learn how to run it."

I'm certain he could have developed his own successful system because he learned well from his dad, but I understand his doubt. The hard thing about building a company from scratch is that you have two big variables: the system, and the people building the system. If both the people and the system are leaky, the chances for failure are great. Sometimes it's hard to know whether the problem is the person or the system that is failing.

Before Franchises

When my rich dad began teaching me about becoming a B, there was only one kind of business—big business, a major corporation that usually dominated the town. In our town in Hawaii, it was the sugar plantation that controlled virtually everything, including other big businesses. So there were big businesses and mom-and-pop S-type businesses, with little in between.

Working at the top levels of those big sugar companies wasn't a realistic goal for people like rich dad and me. Minorities such as the Japanese, Chinese, and Hawaiians worked in the fields, but were never allowed in the boardroom. So rich dad learned everything he knew simply by trial and error.

As I started high school, we began to hear about a thing called "franchises," but none had come to our little town. We hadn't yet heard about McDonald's, Kentucky Fried Chicken, or Taco Bell. They weren't part of our vocabulary while I was studying with rich dad. When we did hear rumors about them, we heard they were illegal, fraudulent scams and dangerous. Rather than believe the rumors, rich dad flew to California to check out franchising for himself. When he returned, all he said was, "Franchises are the wave of the future," and he bought the rights to two of them. His wealth skyrocketed as the idea of franchises caught on, and he began selling his rights to other people so they could have a chance at building their own businesses.

When I asked him if I should buy one from him, he simply said, "No. You've come this far in learning how to build your own business system. Don't stop now. Franchises are for people who don't want to build, or don't know how to build their own systems. Besides, you don't have the $250,000 it takes to buy a franchise from me."

It's hard to imagine today a city without a McDonald's or Burger King or Pizza Hut on every corner. Yet there was a time, not too long ago, when they didn't even exist.

How to Learn to Become a B

The way I learned to become a B was by being an apprentice to my rich dad. His son and I were both E's learning to be B's. And that is the way many people learn. It's called on-the-job training. This is the way many closely-held family empires are passed on from one generation to the next.

The problem is that not too many people are privileged or lucky enough to learn the behind-the-scenes aspects of becoming a B. Most corporate management-training programs are just that—the company only trains you to be a manager. Few teach what it takes to be a B.

Often people get stuck in the S quadrant on their journey to the B quadrant. This happens primarily because they don't develop a strong-enough system and end up becoming an integral part of the system. Successful B's develop a system that will run without their involvement.

There are three ways you can make it to the B side quickly.

1. **Find a mentor.**
   My rich dad was my mentor. A mentor is someone who has already done what you want to do and is successful at doing it. Don't find an advisor. An advisor is someone who tells you how to do it but may not have personally done it. Most advisors are in the S quadrant. The world is filled with S's trying to tell you how to be a B or an I. My rich dad was a mentor, not an advisor. One of the biggest tips my rich dad gave me was this: "Be careful of the advice you take. While you must keep your mind open, always be aware of which quadrant the advice is coming from."

My rich dad taught me about systems and how to be a leader of people, not a manager of people. Managers often see their subordinates as inferiors. Leaders must direct people who are often smarter.

A traditional way of learning about systems is getting your MBA from a prestigious school and then getting a fast-track job that takes you up the corporate ladder. An MBA is important because you learn the basics of accounting and how the financial numbers relate to the systems of a business. Yet having an MBA doesn't mean you're competent to run all the systems that ultimately make up a complete business system.

To learn about all the systems necessary in a big company, you'll need to spend 10 to 15 years there and learn all the different aspects of the business. You should then be prepared to leave and start your own company. Working for a successful major corporation is like being paid by your mentor.

Even with a mentor and/or years of experience, this first method is labor-intensive. Creating your own system requires a lot of trial and error, up-front legal costs, and paperwork. All of this occurs at the same time you're trying to develop your people.

2. *Buy a franchise.*

Another way to learn about systems is to buy a franchise. When you buy a franchise, you're buying a tried-and-proven operating system.

By buying the franchise system, instead of trying to create your own system, you can focus on developing your people. Buying the system removes one big variable when you're learning how to be a B. Many banks will loan money for a franchise, but not for a small start-up business, because they recognize the importance of systems and how starting with a good system lowers their risk.

A word of caution: Franchises are hard for people with an S-quadrant mentality who want to do their own thing. If you buy a franchise system, be an E. Just do it exactly the way they tell you to do it. Nothing is more tragic than the courtroom fights between franchisees and franchisors. The fights happen because the people who buy the system really want to do it their way, not the way the person who created the system wants it done. If you want to do your own thing, then do it after you've mastered both systems and people.

My highly educated dad failed, even though he bought a famous ice cream franchise. Although the system was excellent, the business still failed. In my opinion, the franchise failed because his partners were all E's and S's who didn't know what to do when things started to go bad and didn't ask for support from the parent company. In the end, the partners fought among themselves, and the business went down. They forgot that a true B is more than a system. It's also dependent on good people to operate the system.

Banks Don't Lend Money to People Without Systems

If a bank won't lend money to a small business without a system, why should you? Almost daily, people come to me with business plans with the hope of raising money for their idea or their project.

Most of the time I turn them down for one main reason: The people raising the money don't know the difference between a product and a system. I've had friends ask me to invest money in developing a new music CD, and others who want me to help form a new nonprofit to change the world. As much as I might like the project, the product, or the person, I'll turn them down if they have little or no experience in creating and running business systems.

Just because you can sing doesn't mean you understand the systems of marketing, finance and accounting, sales, human resources, and the many other systems that are required to keep a business afloat and make it successful.

For a business to survive and thrive, 100 percent of all the systems must be functioning and accountable. For example, an airplane is a system of systems. If it takes off and, let's say, the fuel system fails, there often is a crash.

The human body is also a system of systems. Most of us have had a loved one die because one of the body systems failed. The same thing happens in business.

That is why building a tried-and-true business system isn't easy. It's the systems you forget about or don't pay attention to that cause you to crash and burn. That's why I rarely invest with an E or S who has a new product or idea. Professional investors tend to invest in proven systems with people who know how to run those systems.

If banks lend based only on tried-and-true systems and the person who is going to run them, then you should do the same if you want to be a smart investor.

3. ***Get involved in network marketing***
    (also called multi-level marketing or direct distribution systems).
    Just as with franchises, the U.S. legal system initially attempted to outlaw network marketing. It has been banned and restricted in some countries. Any new system or idea often goes through a period of being classified as strange and suspicious. At first, I also thought that network marketing was a scam. But over the years I've studied the various systems available through network marketing, watched several friends become successful at this form of B, and changed my mind.

    After I dropped my prejudices and began researching network marketing, I found many people who were sincerely and diligently building successful network-marketing businesses. When I met these people, I saw the impact their business had on other people's lives and financial futures. I began to truly appreciate the value of the network-marketing system. For a reasonable entry fee (often around $200), people can buy into an existing system and immediately start building their business. Due to the technological advances in the computer industry, these organizations are totally automated, and the headaches of paperwork, order processing, distribution, accounting, and follow-up are almost entirely managed by the network-marketing software systems. New distributors can focus all of their efforts on building their business instead of worrying about the normal start-up headaches of a small business.

One of my old friends who did more than a billion dollars in real estate business in one year, recently signed on as a network-marketing distributor and began building his business. I was surprised to find him so diligently building a network-marketing business because he definitely didn't need the money. When I asked him why, he explained it this way: "I went to school to become a CPA, and I have an MBA in finance. When people ask me how I became so rich, I tell them about the multimillion-dollar real estate transactions I do and the hundreds of thousands of dollars in passive income I receive each year from it. I then notice that some of them withdraw or shy away. We both know that their chances of doing multimillion-dollar real estate investments like I do are slim to none. So I began to look for a way I could help them achieve the same level of passive income I developed from real estate without going back to school for six years and spending 12 years investing in real estate. I believe network marketing gives people the opportunity to build up the passive income they need for support while they learn to become professional investors. That is why I recommend network marketing to them. Even if they have little money, they can still invest 'sweat equity' for five years and begin to generate more than enough passive income to begin investing. By developing their own business, they have the free time to learn, and the capital to invest with me in my bigger deals."

After researching several opportunities, my friend joined a network-marketing company as a distributor and started a network-marketing business with people who might someday want to invest with him. He's now doing well in his network-marketing business, as well as in his investment business. He told me, "I did it initially because I wanted to help people find the money to invest, and now I'm getting rich from a whole new business."

Twice a month, he holds classes on Saturdays. At the first meeting, he teaches people about business systems and people, or how to develop into a successful B. On the second meeting of the month, he teaches them about financial literacy and financial intelligence in order to turn them into savvy I's. His class sizes are growing rapidly.

The pattern he recommends is the same one I recommend.

A Personal Franchise

That's why today I recommend that people consider network marketing. Many famous franchises cost a million dollars or more to buy. Network marketing is like buying a personal franchise, often for less than $200.

I know much of network marketing is hard work. But success in any quadrant is hard work. I personally generate no income as a network-marketing distributor. I researched several network-marketing companies and their compensation plans. While doing my research, I did join several companies, just because their products are so good and I use them as a consumer.

The one recommendation I have for finding a good organization to help you move to the right side of the CASHFLOW Quadrant is to focus not so much on the product, but on the education the organization offers. There are network-marketing organizations that are only interested in having you sell their system to your friends, and there are organizations primarily interested in educating you and helping you succeed.

From my research into network marketing, I found two important things you can learn through their programs that are essential to become a successful B:

1. To be successful, you need to learn to overcome your fear of being rejected and to stop worrying about what other people say and think about you. So many times I've met people who hold themselves back simply because of what their friends might say if they did something different. I know, because I was the same way. Coming from a small town, everyone knew what everyone else was up to. If someone didn't like what you were doing, the whole town heard about it and made your business their business.

   One of the things I told myself over and over was, "What you think of me is none of my business. What is most important is what I think about myself."

One of the reasons my rich dad encouraged me to work in sales for the Xerox Corporation for four years wasn't because he liked copiers, but because he wanted me to overcome my shyness and fear of rejection.

2. To be successful, you must also learn to lead people. Working with different kinds of people is the hardest thing about business. The people I've met who are successful in any business are those who are natural leaders. The ability to get along with and inspire people is a priceless skill, a skill that can be learned.

As I said, the transition from the left side to the right side isn't so much what you do, but who you have to become. If you learn how to handle rejection, how to not be affected by what other people think of you, and how to lead people, you'll find prosperity. So I endorse any network-marketing organization that is primarily committed to developing you as a human being, rather than developing you into a salesperson. I would seek organizations that:

1. Are proven, with a successful track record, a distribution system, and a compensation plan that have been successful for years.

2. Have a business opportunity you can succeed with, believe in, and share confidently with others.

3. Have ongoing, long-term educational programs to develop you as a human being. Self-confidence is vital on the right side of the CASHFLOW Quadrant.

4. Have a strong mentor program. You want to learn from leaders, not advisors. You want to learn from people who are already leaders, who are on the right side, and who want you to succeed.

5. Have people you respect and enjoy being with.

If the organization meets these five criteria, then and only then look at the product. Too many people look at the product instead of the business system and the organization behind the product. In some of the organizations I looked into, their pitch was, "The product sells itself. It's easy." If you're looking to be a salesperson, an S, then the product is the most important thing. But if you're developing into a long-term B, then the system, lifelong education, and the people are more important.

A friend and colleague of mine who is knowledgeable in this industry reminded me about the value of time, one of our most precious assets.

A true success story in a network-marketing company is when your commitment of time and hard work in the short term results in significant long-term passive income. Once you've built a strong organization below you, you can stop working and your revenue stream will continue from the efforts of the organization you've built. The most important key to success with a network-marketing company is a long-term commitment on your part, as well as the organization's part, in order to mold you into the business leader you want to become.

A System Is a Bridge to Freedom

Being homeless was not an experience I want to repeat. Yet for Kim and me, the experience was priceless. Today, freedom and security are found, not so much in what we have, but in what we know we can create with confidence.

Since that time, we have created or helped develop a real estate company, an oil company, a mining company, and two education companies. So the process of learning how to create a successful system was beneficial for us. Yet I don't recommend the process to anyone unless they truly want to go through it.

Until only a few years ago, the possibility of a person becoming successful in the B quadrant was only available to those who were brave or rich. Kim and I must have been brave, because we certainly weren't rich. Many people stay stuck on the left side because they feel the risks involved in developing their own system are too great. For them, it's smarter to remain safe and secure in a job.

Today, primarily due to changes in technology, the risk in becoming a successful business owner is greatly reduced, and the opportunity to build your own or leverage an existing business system is available to virtually everyone.

Franchises and network marketing took away the hard part of developing your own system. You acquire the rights to a proven system, and then your only job is to develop your people.

Think of business systems as bridges that provide a path for you to cross safely from the left side to the right side of the CASHFLOW Quadrant.

Chapter Five
THE FIVE LEVELS OF INVESTORS

Investing is the key to financial freedom.

My poor dad often said, "Investing is risky."

My rich dad often said, "Being financially uneducated is risky."

Today, most people know they should invest. The problem is that most people, like my poor dad, believe investing is risky—and investing is risky if you lack financial education, experience, and guidance.

Learning to invest is important because investing is the key to financial freedom. Five things happen to people who do not invest, or who invest poorly:

1. They work hard all their lives.
2. They worry about money all their lives.
3. They depend on others, such as family, a company pension, or the government, to take care of them.

4. The boundaries of their lives are defined by money.

5. They will not know what true freedom is.

Rich dad often said, "You will never know true freedom until you achieve financial freedom." By this, he meant that learning to invest is more important than learning a profession. He said, "When you learn a profession, let's say to be a doctor, you learn how to work for money. Learning to invest is learning how to have money work for you. The moment you have money working for you, you have your ticket to freedom." He also said, "The more money you have working for you, the less you pay in taxes—if you are a true investor."

Learning to Invest

My rich dad began preparing me for the I quadrant at the age of nine using the game of *Monopoly*® as a teaching tool. Over and over again, he would say, "One of the great formulas for wealth is found in the game of *Monopoly*. Always remember the formula: four green houses, one red hotel."

The game of *Monopoly* is a game of cash flow. For example, if you had one green house on a property you owned and you received $10, that was $10 a month in cash flow. Two houses, $20. Three houses, $30. And the red hotel, $50. More green houses and more red hotels mean more cash flow, less work, less taxes, and more freedom.

A simple game—but an important lesson.

Rich dad played *Monopoly* in real life. He would often take his son and me to visit his green houses—green houses that would one day become a big red hotel, right on Waikiki Beach.

As I grew up and watched my rich dad play the game of *Monopoly* in real life, I learned many valuable lessons about investing. Some of those lessons are:

- Investing is not risky.

- Investing is fun.

- Investing can make you very, very, rich.

- More importantly, investing can set you free—free from the struggle of earning a living and worrying about money.

In other words, if you were smart, you could build a pipeline of cash flow for life—a pipeline that would produce cash in good times and bad, in market booms and market crashes. Your cash flow would increase automatically with inflation and, at the same time, allow you to pay less in taxes.

I am not saying real estate is the only way to invest. I use the game of *Monopoly* simply as an example of how the rich get richer. A person can earn income from stocks via dividends, from bonds via interest, or from oil, books, and patents via royalties. In other words, there are many ways to financial freedom.

Financial "Experts"

Unfortunately, due to a lack of financial education in schools, most people blindly turn their money over to people they believe are financial experts: people such as bankers, financial planners, and stockbrokers. Unfortunately, most of these "experts" are not really investors in the I quadrant. Most are employees in the E quadrant working for a paycheck, or self-employed financial advisors in the S quadrant working for fees and commissions. Most "experts" cannot afford to stop working, simply because they don't have investments working for them.

Warren Buffett said, "Wall Street is the only place that people ride to in a Rolls Royce, to get advice from those who take the subway."

If people do not have sound financial education, they cannot tell if a financial advisor is a salesman or a con man, a fool or a genius. Remember, all con men are nice people. If they were not being nice by telling you what you want to hear, you would not listen to them.

There is nothing wrong with being a sales person. We all have something to sell. Yet, as Warren Buffet says, "Never ask an insurance salesman if you need insurance." When it comes to money, there are many people desperate enough to tell and sell you anything, just to get your money.

Interestingly, the vast majority of investors never meet the person taking their money. In most of the Western world, employees simply have their money automatically deducted from their paycheck, the same way the tax department collects taxes. Many workers in America simply allow their employer to deduct their money and put it into their 401(k) retirement plan, possibly the worst way to invest for retirement. *(401(k) plans go by different names in different countries. In Australia they are called superannuation plans, in Japan they are also called 401(k)s, and in Canada they are known as RRSPs.)*

I say the 401(k) may possibly be the worst way to invest for retirement for the following reasons:

1. **TIME** *magazine is on my side.*

   TIME magazine has run a number of articles over the years, questioning the wisdom of putting so many people's retirement at risk. *TIME* has been predicting that millions will not have enough money to retire after a lifetime of turning their money over to strangers.

   A typical 401(k) plan takes 80 percent of the profits. The investor may receive 20 percent, if they are lucky. The investor puts up 100 percent of the money and takes 100 percent of the risk. The 401(k) plan puts up 0 percent of the money and takes 0 percent of the risk. The 401(k) company makes money, even if you lose money.

2. *Taxes work against you with a 401(k).*
   Long-term capital gains are taxed at a lower rate of around 15%. But the 401(k) gains are taxed at the ordinary earned income-tax rate

of around 35%, the highest of the three types of income, which are:

- Ordinary earned

- Portfolio

- Passive

If you want to take the money out of your 401(k) early, you'll have to pay an additional 10% penalty tax.

3. **You have no insurance if there is a stock-market crash.**
To drive a car, I must have insurance in case there is a crash. When I invest in real estate, I have insurance in case of fire or other losses. Yet the 401(k) investor has no insurance to prevent losses from market crashes.

4. **The 401(k) is for people who are planning to be poor when they retire.**
That is why financial planners often say, "When you retire, you'll be taxed at a lower tax rate." They assume your income will go down in retirement into a lower tax bracket. If, on the other hand, you are rich when you retire and you have a 401(k), you could pay even higher taxes at retirement. Smart investors understand taxes before investing.

The sad truth about most financial advisors and pension-fund managers is that they are not investors.

Most are employees in the E quadrant. One reason why so many government pensions and union pensions are in trouble is because these employees are not trained to be investors. Most do not have any real-life financial education.

To make matters worse, most financial "experts" advise uneducated investors to "invest for the long term in a well-diversified portfolio of stocks, bonds, and mutual funds."

Why do these financial "experts," employees in the E quadrant or sales people in the S quadrant masquerading as investors in the I quadrant, advise you to do that? It's because they get paid, not by how much money they make for you, but by how much money you turn over to them for the long term. The longer your money is parked with them, the more they get paid.

The reality is that real investors do not park their money. They move their money. It is a strategy known as the "velocity of money." A true investor's money is always moving, acquiring new assets, and then moving on to acquire even more assets. Only amateurs park their money.

I am not saying 401(k)-type plans are bad, although I would never have one. For me, they are too expensive, too risky, too tax-inefficient, and unfair to the investor.

I am saying there are better ways to invest, but they require financial education.

What Is the Best Investment?

The average investor does not know the difference between investing for cash flow and investing for capital gains. Most investors invest for capital gains, hoping and praying the price of their stock or home goes up. As long as you have more cash flowing in than flowing out, your investment is a good investment.

Keep in mind that it's not the asset class that makes a person rich or poor. For example, when a person asks, "Is real estate is a good investment?" I reply, "I don't know. Are you a good investor?" Or if they ask, "Are stocks a good investment?" again my answer is the same, "I don't know. Are you a good investor?"

My point is that it is never the investment or asset class that is important. Success or failure, wealth or poverty, depends solely on how smart the investor is. A smart investor will make millions in the stock market. An amateur will lose millions.

Tragically, most people do not think learning to invest is important. This is why most people believe investing is risky and turn their money over to "experts," most of whom are not really investors, but sales people who make money whether the investor makes money or loses money.

Five Different Levels of Investors

There are five types or levels of investors found in the I quadrant.

Level 1: The Zero-Financial-Intelligence Level

Sadly, in America, once the richest country in the world, over 50 percent of the U.S. population is at the bottom level of the I quadrant. Simply said, they have nothing to invest.

There are many people who make a lot of money who fall into this category. They earn a lot—and spend more than they earn.

I have a friend who looks very rich. He has a good job as a real estate broker, a beautiful wife, and three kids in private school. They live in a beautiful house overlooking the Pacific Ocean in San Diego. He and his wife drive expensive European cars. When his son and daughters were old enough, they too drove expensive cars. They looked rich, but what they had was bad debt. They looked rich, but were poorer than most poor people.

Now, they are homeless. When the real estate market crashed, they crashed. They were no longer able to pay the interest on all the debt they had accumulated.

When we were younger, this same friend made a lot of money. Unfortunately, it was his low financial-intelligence level—zero—that caused him be a zero over the long run. In fact, he is so deeply in debt that he is really a sub-zero investor.

Like many people, everything he buys loses value or costs him money. Nothing he buys makes him richer.

Level 2: The Savers-Are-Losers Level

Many people believe it is smart to save money. The problem is that today, "money" is no longer money. Today, people are saving counterfeit dollars, money that can be created at the speed of light.

In 1971 President Nixon took the U.S. dollar off the gold standard, and money became debt. The primary reason why prices have risen since 1971 is simply because the United States now has the power to print money to pay its bills.

Today, savers are the biggest losers. Since 1971, the U.S. dollar has lost 95 percent of its value when compared to gold. It will not take another 40 years to lose its remaining 5 percent.

Remember, in 1971, gold was $35 an ounce. Forty years later, gold was $1,400 an ounce. That is a massive loss of purchasing power for the dollar. The problem grows worse as the U.S. national debt escalates into the trillions of dollars and the U.S. continues to print more "counterfeit" money.

As the Federal Reserve Bank and central banks throughout the world print trillions of dollars at high speed, every printed dollar means higher taxes and more inflation. In spite of this fact, millions of people continue to believe saving money is smart. It used to be smart when money was money.

The biggest market in the world is the bond market. "Bond" is another word for "savings." There are many different types of bonds for different types of savers. There are U.S. Treasury bonds, corporate bonds, municipal bonds, and junk bonds.

For years, it was assumed that U.S. government bonds and government municipal bonds were safe. Then the financial crisis of 2007 began. As many of you know, the crisis was caused by mortgage bonds such as mortgage-backed securities or MBS, also known as derivatives. Millions of these mortgage bonds were made up of subprime mortgages, which were loans to subprime or high-risk borrowers. You may recall that some of those borrowers had no income and no job. Yet, they were buying homes they could never pay for.

The Wall Street bankers took these subprime loans and packaged them into bonds, magically got this subprime bond labeled as prime, and sold them to institutions, banks, governments, and individual investors. To me, this is fraud. But that is the banking system.

Once the subprime borrower could no longer pay the interest on their mortgages, these MBS bonds began blowing up all over the world.

Interestingly, it was Warren Buffett's firm, Moody's, that blessed these subprime mortgages as AAA prime debt, the highest rating for bonds.

Today, many people blame the big banks, such as Goldman Sachs and J.P. Morgan, for the crisis. Yet if anyone should be blamed for this crisis, it should be Warren Buffet. He is a smart man, and he knew what he was doing. Moody's was blessing rotting dog meat as Grade A prime beef. That is criminal.

The problem is that these subprime bonds are now causing ripple effects all over the world. Today, countries such as Ireland and Greece are in serious trouble, unable to pay the interest on their bonds. In the United States, governments and municipalities are going broke, unable to pay the interest on their bonds.

In 2011, millions of individuals, many retirees, pension funds, governments, and banks are in trouble as the bond market proves how unsafe bonds can be.

On top of that, rising inflation makes bonds an even riskier investment, which is why savers who only know how to save are losers. For example, if a bond is paying 3 percent interest and inflation is running at 5 percent, the value of a 3 percent bond crashes, wiping out investors' value.

China could be the biggest loser of all. China holds a trillion dollars in U.S. bonds. Every time the U.S. government devalues the dollar by printing more money and issuing more bonds, the value of China's trillion-dollar investment in the United States goes down. If China stops buying U.S. government bonds, the world economy will stop and crash.

Millions of retirees are just like China. Retirees in need of a steady income after retirement believed government bonds were safe. Today, as governments, big and small, go bust and inflation rises, retirees are finding out that savers who saved money in bonds are losers.

Municipal bonds are IOUs issued by states, cities, hospitals, schools, and other public institutions. One advantage of municipal bonds is that many are tax-free income. The problem is that municipal bonds are not risk-free.

Millions of municipal-bond investors are now finding out that the municipal bonds they invested in are in serious trouble. In the United States, more than $3 trillion is invested in municipal bonds. It is estimated that two thirds of those bonds are now at risk because these public institutions are broke. If more money is not pumped in, the United States could implode from the center as states, cities, hospitals, and schools begin to default, just as subprime homeowners defaulted and stopped paying on their home mortgages.

The bond market is the biggest market in the world, bigger than the stock market or the real estate market. The main reason it is the biggest is because most people are savers—Level-2 investors. Unfortunately, after 1971 when the rules of money changed, savers became the biggest losers, even if they saved money by investing in bonds.

Remember that savers, bondholders, and most people who save money in a retirement plan, are people who park their money, investing for the long term, while professional investors move their money. Professional investors invest their money in an asset, get their money back without selling the asset, and move their money on to buy more assets. That is why savers who park their money are the biggest losers.

Level 3: The I'm-Too-Busy Level

This is the investor that is too busy to learn about investing. Many investors at this level are highly educated people who are simply too busy with their careers, family, other interests, and vacations. Hence, they prefer to remain financially naïve and turn their money over to someone else to manage for them.

This is the level that most 401(k), IRA, and even very rich investors are at. They simply turn their money over to an "expert," and then hope and pray their expert is really an expert.

Soon after the financial crisis broke in 2007, many affluent people found out that their trusted expert was not an expert at all and, even worse, could not be trusted.

In a matter of months, trillions of dollars of wealth vaporized as real estate and stock markets began to crash. Panicking, these investors called their trusted advisors and begged for salvation.

A few rich investors found out that their trusted advisors were extremely sophisticated con men, running elaborate Ponzi schemes. A Ponzi scheme is an investment scheme where investors are paid off with new investors' money. The scheme works well as long as there are new investors adding new money to pay off the old investors. In the United States, Bernie Madoff became famous because he "made off" with billions in rich people's money.

There are legal Ponzi schemes and illegal Ponzi schemes. Social Security is a legal Ponzi scheme, as is the stock market. In both instances, the scheme works as long as new money flows into the scheme. If new money stops flowing in, the scheme—be it Madoff's scheme, Social Security, or Wall Street—collapses.

The problem with the Level-3 investor, the I'm-too-busy investor, is that the person learns nothing if they lose their money. They have no experience except a bad experience. All they can do is blame their advisor, the market, or the government. It is hard to learn from one's mistakes if the person does not know what mistakes were made.

Level 4: The I'm-a-Professional Level

This is the do-it-yourself investor in the S quadrant. Many retirees become Level-4 investors once their working days are over.

This investor may buy and sell a few stocks, often from a discount broker. After all, why should they pay a stockbroker's higher commissions when they can do their own research and make their own decisions?

If they invest in real estate, the do-it-yourselfer will find, fix, and manage their own properties. And if the person is a gold bug, they will buy and store their own gold and silver.

In most cases, the do-it-yourselfer has very little, if any, formal financial education. After all, if they can do it themselves, why should they learn anything?

If they do attend a course or two, it is often in a narrow subject area. For example, if they like stock trading, they will focus only on stock trading. The same is true for the small real estate investor.

At the age of nine, when rich dad began my financial education with the game of *Monopoly*, he wanted me to have a bigger picture of the world of investing. The following are some of the basic big-picture asset classes he wanted me to spend my life learning.

Assets	Liabilities
Business **Real Estate** **Paper** **Commodities**	

As more people realize the need to invest, millions of them will become small Level-4 investors in all four categories.

After the 2007 market crash, millions of people have become entrepreneurs starting small businesses, and many are investing in real estate while prices are low. Most, however, are trying their hand at stock trading and stock picking. As the dollar declines in value, millions of people are beginning to save gold and silver instead of dollars.

Obviously, those who also invest in their ongoing financial education, taking classes regularly and hiring a coach to enhance their performance, will outpace those who just do it on their own.

With a sound financial education, a few of the Level-4 investors will climb to the next level, the Level-5 investor, the capitalist.

Level 5: The Capitalist Level

This is the richest-people-in-the-world level. The Level-5 investor, a capitalist, is a business owner from the B quadrant investing in the I quadrant.

As stated earlier, the Level-4 investor is the do-it-yourselfer from the S quadrant investing in the I quadrant.

The following are a few examples of the differences between a Level-4 investor and a Level-5 capitalist investor.

1. The S-quadrant investor generally uses his or her own money to invest.

   The B-quadrant investor generally uses OPM (other people's money) to invest.

   This difference is one of the major differences between the Level-4 and Level-5 investor.

2. The S-quadrant investor is often a solo investor. (The S also stands for smartest.)

   The B-quadrant investor invests with a team. B-quadrant investors do not have to be the smartest. They just have to have the smartest team.

Most people know that two minds are better than one. Yet, many S-quadrant investors believe they are the smartest people in the world.

3. The S-quadrant investor earns less than the B-quadrant investor.

4. The S-quadrant investor often pays higher taxes than the B-quadrant investor.

5. The S quadrant also stands for selfish. The more selfish they are, the more money they make.

   The B-quadrant investor must be generous. The more generous they are, the more money they make.

6. It is difficult to raise money as an S-quadrant investor. It is easy for a B-quadrant investor to raise capital. Once a person knows how to build a business in the B quadrant, success attracts money. It becomes easy to raise money in the I quadrant if you are successful in the B quadrant. That is the big "if."

The ease of raising capital is one of the biggest differences between being successful in the S quadrant versus being successful in the B quadrant. Once a person is successful in the B quadrant, life is easy. The challenge is becoming successful.

The problem with success in the S quadrant is that raising capital is always difficult.

For example, it is easy to take a B-quadrant business public via selling shares of the business on the stock market. The story of Facebook is a modern example of how easy it is to raise capital for a B-quadrant business. If Facebook had remained just a small web-consulting firm, it would have been very difficult to raise investor capital.

Another example is McDonald's. If McDonald's had remained just a single hamburger store, an S-quadrant operation, no one would have invested in it. Once McDonald's began expanding into the B quadrant via a franchise system and was listed on the stock exchange, money poured in.

The reason a business sells "shares" is because the more they share, the richer the entrepreneur becomes. An S-quadrant business has a tough time selling shares because the business is too small to share.

In real estate, the same is true. When I was a small real estate investor investing in single-family homes, condos, and small 4- to 30-unit apartment buildings, it was difficult getting loans.

The moment Kim and I began investing in apartment buildings with over 100 units, banks were more willing to lend us much more money. The reason? On 100-unit-plus properties priced in the millions, banks do not finance the investor. They finance the investment. In other words, on properties with over 100 units, banks look more closely at the investment than the investor.

On top of that, bankers would rather lend $10 million than$10,000 since it takes just as much time to lend thousands as it does millions. Remember, bankers love debtors because debtors make the bank rich.

Once bankers are satisfied with our ability to own and manage large apartment houses profitably, banks often line up to offer us money, even during a crisis.

So the question is: Who do Level-5 investors get their money from? The answer is: They get their money from Level-2 and Level-3 investors who save their money in banks and pension plans.

Starting with Nothing

The reason I started this book with the story of Kim and me being homeless is to let readers know that not having any money is not an excuse for not growing smarter, thinking bigger, and becoming richer.

For most of my life, I have never had enough money. If I had let not having money be an excuse, I would never have become a capitalist. This is important, because a true capitalist never has money. That is why they must know how to raise capital and use other people's money to make a lot of money for a lot of people.

How to Become a Capitalist

My mom and dad wanted me to be successful in the E and S quadrants. My dad suggested I go to school, get my PhD, which he did himself, and work for the government or climb a corporate ladder in the E quadrant. My mom, a registered nurse, wanted me to become a medical doctor in the S quadrant.

My rich dad suggested I become a capitalist. That meant I had to study the skills required for success in the B and I quadrants.

My mom and dad believed in traditional schools such as colleges, law schools, and medical schools. They valued good grades, degrees, and credentials, such as a law degree or a medical license.

My rich dad believed in education, but not the type of education found in traditional schools. Rather than go to school, my rich dad signed up for seminars and courses that improved his business and investing skills. He also took personal-development courses. He was not interested in grades or credentials. He wanted real-life skills that gave him strengths and operational skills in the B and I quadrants.

When I was in high school, my rich dad often flew to Honolulu to attend seminars on entrepreneurship and investing. One day, when I told my poor dad that rich dad was going to a class on sales, my poor dad laughed. He could not understand why anyone would want to learn how to sell, especially if the class hours were not applied as credit to an advanced college degree. My poor dad also looked down upon my rich dad because my rich dad never finished high school.

Because I had two dads with differing attitudes on education, I became aware that there is more than one type of education. Traditional schools are for those who want to be successful in the E and S quadrants. Another type of education is for those who want to be successful in the B and I quadrants.

In 1973, I returned from Vietnam. It was time for me to make up my mind about which dad I was going to follow. Was I going to follow in my poor dad's footsteps and go back to school to become an E or an S, or take my rich dad's path and become a B or an I, eventually to become a capitalist?

In 1973, my rich dad suggested I take classes on real estate investing. He said, "If you want to be a successful capitalist, you must know how to raise capital and how to use debt to make money."

That year I took a three-day workshop on real estate investing. It was the start of my education into the world of the capitalist.

A few months later, after looking at over 100 properties, I purchased my first rental property on the island of Maui, using 100 percent debt financing and still putting $25 cash flow in my pocket each month. My real-life education had begun. I was learning to use other people's money to make money, a skill a true capitalist must know.

In 1974, my contract with the Marine Corps was up, and I took a job with the Xerox Corporation in Hawaii, not because I wanted to climb the corporate ladder, but because Xerox had the best sales-training program. Again, this was all part of my rich dad's educational program to train me to become a capitalist.

By 1994, Kim and I were financially free, never needing a job or a company or a government retirement plan. Rich dad was correct. My education could set me free—but not the education found in traditional schools.

When the markets began to crash in 2007, rather than crash with the rest of the economy, our wealth skyrocketed. As the stock market and real estate markets crashed, great deals floated to the surface, and banks were more than eager to lend us millions of dollars to buy and take over their investments gone bad. In 2010 alone, Kim and I acquired over $87 million in real estate, using loans from banks and pension funds. That year was our best year so far.

As rich dad often said, "If you are a true investor, it does not matter if the markets are going up or coming down. A true investor does well in any market condition."

Where Are You?

Take a moment and assess where you are today.

Are You at Investor Level 1?

If there is nothing in your asset column with no income coming in from your investments and you have too many liabilities, then you are starting at the bottom level, ground zero.

If you are deeply in bad debt, your best investment might be to get out of debt. There is nothing wrong with being deeply in debt, unless you do nothing. After I lost my first business, I was nearly a million dollars in debt. It took me almost five years to reach zero. In many ways, learning from my mistakes and taking responsibility for my mistakes was the best education I could have asked for. If I had not learned from my mistakes, I would not be where I am today.

Kim and I put together a simple program and workbook, *How We Got Out of Bad Debt,* explaining the process we used to get out of hundreds of thousands of dollars of bad debt. It is a simple, almost painless, process. All it takes is some discipline and a willingness to learn.

Are You at Investor Level 2?

If you are a saver, be very careful, especially if you are saving money in a bank or in a retirement plan. In general, savers are losers.

Saving is often a strategy for people who do not want to learn anything. You see, it takes no financial intelligence to save. You can train a monkey to save money.

The risk in saving is that you learn little. And if your savings are wiped out, either by market decline or devaluation of the money supply, you wind up without money and without education.

Remember that the U.S. dollar has lost 95 percent of its value since 1971. It will not take long to lose the rest of its value.

As stated before, a person can even lose money saving gold if they buy gold at the wrong price.

I suggest taking a few courses on investing, either in stocks or real estate, and see if anything interests you. If nothing interests you, then keep saving.

Remember that the bond market is the biggest market in the world simply because most people and businesses are savers, not investors. This may sound strange to savers, but the bond market and banks need borrowers.

Are You at Investor Level 3?

This level is similar to Level 2, except that this level invests in riskier instruments such as stocks, bonds, mutual funds, insurance, and exchange-traded funds.

Again, the risk with this level is that, if everything is lost, the investor loses everything—and learns nothing.

If you are ready to move out of Level 3 by investing in your financial education and taking control of your money, then Level 4 is a good level for you.

Are You at Investor Level 4?

If you are here as a professional investor, congratulations. Very few people invest the time to learn and manage their own money. The key to success at Level 4 is lifelong learning, great teachers, great coaches, and like-minded friends.

Level-4 investors take control of their lives, knowing that their mistakes are their opportunities to learn and to grow.

The fear of investing does not frighten them. It challenges them.

Are You at Investor Level 5?

To me, being a capitalist investor at level 5 is like being on top of the world. Literally, the world is your oyster. The world has no borders. In this world of high-speed technology, it is easier than ever to be a capitalist in a world of plenty.

If you are at this level, keep learning and keep giving. Remember that true capitalists are generous because a B-quadrant capitalist knows you must give more to receive more.

It's Your Choice

One great thing about freedom is the freedom to choose to live the life you want to live.

In 1973 at the age of 26, I knew I did not want to live my life the way my parents chose to live. I did not want to be living below my means, living paycheck to paycheck, trying to make ends meet. To me, this was not living. It may have been good for them, but I knew in my heart that it was not right for me.

I also knew that going back to school for advanced degrees was not for me. I knew school did not make people rich because I grew up in a family of advanced degrees. Most of my uncles and aunts had masters degrees and a few had their doctorates.

I did not want to climb a corporate ladder in the E quadrant either, nor did I want to be a very special specialist in the S quadrant.

So I took the path less traveled and decided to become an entrepreneur and professional investor. I wanted the freedom to travel the world, do business, and invest.

It was my choice. I do not recommend that path for everyone. But I do recommend that a person choose. That is what freedom is—the power to choose.

I encourage you to look at the five levels of investors and make your choice. Each level has its pros and cons, its advantages and disadvantages. Each level has a price greater than money.

If you choose Level 1, 2, or 3, there are many other people and organizations qualified to support your investment life at those levels.

In 1997 Kim and I created The Rich Dad Company to provide educational games, programs, and coaches for those individuals who seek to be Level-4 and Level-5 investors.

A Final Word on Investing

In the world of money, you will often see the term ROI, Return On Investment. Depending upon whom you talk to, ROI will vary. For example, if you talk to a banker, he or she may say, "We pay 3 percent interest on your money." For many people, this may sound good. If you talk to a financial planner, they may say, "You can expect a return on your investment of 10 percent per year." To many people, a 10 percent return is exciting.

To most people, especially those in the E and S quadrants, the higher your return, the greater the risk. So the person accepting a 10 percent return already assumes there is more risk in that investment than the 3 percent return from the bank. And there is.

Ironically, both the 3 percent return from the bank and the 10 percent return from the stock market are extremely high-risk. The money in the bank is at risk due to inflation and higher taxes caused by banks printing money. The 10 percent in the stock market is at risk due to volatility caused by HFT (high-frequency trading) and due to the novice investor investing without insurance.

In my world, ROI stands for a Return On Information. This means that the more information I have, the higher my returns—and the lower my risk.

I caution you, because what I am about to say may sound insane or too good to be true. Yet I assure you, it is true.

In my world, the world of a Level-4 and Level-5 investor, an infinite return is expected—and with low risk. An infinite return means "money for nothing." In other words, investors receive income without having any of their own money in the investment.

In an earlier section, I wrote that I took a real estate course in 1973. After looking at over 100 investments, I purchased a condo on Maui using 100 percent financing, which means I used none of my own money. I put $25 each month into my pocket. That $25 was an infinite return on my investment, since I had zero invested. And I quote from that section, "My real-life education had begun. I was learning to use other people's money to make money, a skill a true capitalist must know."

I know $25 a month is not a lot of money. Yet, it was not the money that was important to me. It was learning a way of thinking, a way of processing information and producing a result.

One of the reasons that I have so much money today is simply because I was educated and trained to think differently. If you have read *Rich Dad Poor Dad,* you may recall that the title of the first chapter is "The Rich Don't Work for Money." One of the reasons why those in the E and S quadrants have problems with that statement is because most went to school to learn to work for money. They did not go to school to learn how to have other people's money work for them.

When Kim and I started The Rich Dad Company, we borrowed $250,000 from investors. We paid the money back once the company was up and running. Today, the business has returned multi-millions of dollars, not only to Kim and me, but to companies and individuals associated with Rich Dad. As I said, capitalists are generous.

My point is that, the moment a person knows how to make money out of nothing or with other people's money or a bank's money, they enter a different world. It's a world almost exactly opposite from the E and S quadrants' world of hard work, high taxes, and low returns on investment.

The reason most people believe saving is smart and a 10 percent return in the stock market is worth it is simply due to a lack of financial education.

Your best ROI is not a return on your investment, but a return on your information. This is why a financial education is essential, especially for the uncertainty of the world ahead.

Remember this about the word *education*: "Education gives us the power to turn information into meaning." In the Information Age, we are drenched with financial information. Yet, without financial education, we cannot turn information into useful meaning for our lives.

In closing, I say the I quadrant is the most important quadrant for your future. No matter what you do for a living, how well you do in the I quadrant will determine your future. In other words, even if you make very little money in the E or S quadrant, financial education in the I quadrant is your ticket to freedom and financial security.

For example, my sister is a Buddhist nun. She earns nearly zero in the S quadrant. Yet she attends our investment courses and has steadily been increasing her financial education. Today, her future is bright because she stopped saving money in the bank and buying mutual funds and began investing in real estate and silver. In the ten years between 2000 and 2010, she has made much more money in the I quadrant than she could ever make as a nun in the S quadrant.

I am very proud of my sister. She may be a nun by profession, but she does not have to be a poor nun.

Before Reading Further

Before we go on, here's the big question:

1.   What level of investor are you?

_____

If you are truly sincere about getting wealthy quickly, read and reread the five levels. Each time I read the levels, I see a little of myself in all the levels. I recognize not only strengths, but also character flaws that hold me back. The way to great financial wealth is to strengthen your strengths and address your character flaws. And the way to do that is by first recognizing them rather than pretending that you're perfect.

We all want to think the best of ourselves. I've dreamed of being a Level-5 capitalist for most of my life. I knew this was what I wanted to become from the moment my rich dad explained the similarities between a stock picker and a person who bets on horses. But after studying the different levels of this list, I could see the character flaws that held me back. I found character flaws in myself from Level 4 that would often rear their ugly heads in times of pressure. The gambler in me was good, but it was also not so good. So with the guidance of Kim, my friends and additional schooling, I began addressing my own character flaws and turning them into strengths. My effectiveness as a Level-5 investor improved immediately.

Although I do operate today as a Level-5 investor, I continue to read and reread the five levels and work on improving myself.

Here's another question for you:

2. *What level of investor do you want or need to be in the near future?*

_____

Warning

Anyone with the goal of becoming a Level-5 Investor must develop their skills FIRST as a Level-4 investor. Level 4 cannot be skipped on your path to Level 5. Anyone who tries to do this is really a Level-3 investor— a gambler!

If your answer to question two is the same as that in question one, then you are where you want to be. If you are happy where you are as an investor, then there's not much need to read any further in this book. One of life's greatest joys is to be happy where you are. Congratulations!

However, if you still want and need to know more financially and continue to be interested in pursuing your financial freedom, read on. The remaining chapters will focus primarily on the characteristics of someone in the B and I quadrants. In these chapters, you will learn how to move from the left side of the CASHFLOW Quadrant to the right side easily and with low risk. The shift from the left side to the right will continue to focus on intangible assets that make possible the tangible assets on the right side.

Before going on, I have one last question:

3. *To go from homeless to millionaires in less than 10 years, what level of investor do you think Kim and I had to be?*

_____

The answer is found in the next chapter where I share some learning experiences from our personal journey to financial freedom.

Chapter Six

YOU CANNOT SEE MONEY WITH YOUR EYES

Money is an idea that is more clearly seen with your mind.

In late 1974, I purchased a small condominium on the fringes of Waikiki as one of my first investment properties. The price was $56,000 for a cute two-bedroom, one-bath unit in an average building. It was a perfect rental unit, and I knew it would rent quickly.

I drove to my rich dad's office, all excited about showing him the deal. He glanced at the documents and, in less than a minute, he looked up and asked, "How much money are you losing a month?"

"About $100 a month," I said.

"Don't be foolish," rich dad said. "I haven't gone over the numbers, but I can already tell from the written documents that you're losing much more than that. And besides, why in the world would you knowingly invest in something that loses money?"

"Well, the unit looked nice, and I thought it was a good deal. A little paint and the place would be as good as new," I said.

"That doesn't justify knowingly losing money," smirked rich dad.

"Well, my real estate agent said not to worry about losing money every month. He said that, in a few years, the price of this unit will double. In addition, the government gives me a tax break on the money I lose. Besides, it was such a good deal that I was afraid someone else would buy it if I didn't."

Rich dad stood and closed his office door. When he did that, I knew I was about to be chewed out as well as be taught an important lesson. I'd been through these types of educational sessions before.

"So how much money are you losing a month?" rich dad asked again.

"About $100," I repeated nervously.

Rich dad shook his head as he scanned the documents. The lesson was about to begin. On that day, I learned more about money and investing than I had in all my previous 27 years of life. Rich dad was happy that I took the initiative and invested in a property, but I'd made some grave mistakes that could have been a financial disaster. However, the lessons I learned from that one investment have made me millions over the years.

Money Is Seen with Your Mind

"It's not what your eyes see," said rich dad. "A piece of real estate is a piece of real estate. A company's stock certificate is a company's stock certificate. You can see those things. But it's what you can't see that's important.

It's the deal, the financial agreement, the market, the management, the risk factors, the cash flow, the corporate structuring, the tax laws, and a thousand other things that make something a good investment or not."

He then proceeded to tear the deal apart with questions. "Why would you pay such a high interest rate? What do you figure your return on investment to be? How does this investment fit into your long-term financial strategy? What vacancy factor are you using? What is your cap rate? Have you checked the association's history of assessments? Have you figured in management costs? What percentage rate did you use to compute repairs? Did you know that the city has just announced it will be tearing up the roads in that area and changing the traffic pattern? A major thoroughfare will run right in front of your building. Residents are moving to avoid the year-long project. Did you know that? I know the market trend is up today, but do you know what is driving that trend—business economics or greed? How long do you think the trend will continue up? What happens if this place doesn't rent? And if it doesn't, how long can you keep this place and yourself afloat? And again, what goes on in your head to make you think that losing money is a good deal? This really has me worried."

"It looked like a good deal," I said, deflated.

Rich dad smiled, stood up, and shook my hand. "I'm glad you took action," he said. "Most people think, but never do. If you do something, you make mistakes, and it's from our mistakes that we learn the most. Remember that anything important can't really be learned in the classroom. It must be learned by taking action, making mistakes, and then correcting them. That's when wisdom sets in."

I felt a little better and was ready to learn.

Rich dad went on to explain that people look at a piece of real estate, or the name of a stock, and often make their decision based on what their eyes see, what a broker tells them or on a hot tip from a fellow worker. They often buy emotionally instead of rationally.

"That's why nine out of 10 investors don't make money," said rich dad. "While they might not lose money, they don't make any either. They just sort of break even, making some and losing some. That's because they invest with their eyes and emotions rather than with their minds. Many people invest because they want to get rich quickly. So instead of becoming investors, they wind up being dreamers, hustlers, gamblers, and crooks. The world is filled with them. So let's sit down, go back over this losing deal you just bought, and I'll teach you how to turn it into a winning deal. I'll begin to teach your mind to see what your eyes can't."

From Bad to Good

The next morning I went back to the real estate agent, rejected the deal as it stood and reopened negotiation. It wasn't a pleasant process, but I learned a lot.

Three days later, I returned to see rich dad. The price of the condo stayed the same, and the agent got his full commission because he deserved it. But while the price remained the same, the terms of the investment were vastly different. By renegotiating the interest rate, payment terms, and the amortization period, instead of losing money, I was now certain of making a net profit of $80 per month, even after the management fee and an allowance for vacancy was factored in. I could even lower my rent and still make money if the market went bad. I could definitely raise the rent if the market got better.

"I estimated that you were going to lose at least $150 per month," said rich dad. "Probably more. If you had continued to lose $150 per month based on your salary and expenses, how many of these deals could you afford?"

"Barely one," I replied. "Most months, I don't have an extra $150. If I had done the original deal, I would have struggled financially every month, even after the tax breaks. I might even have had to take an extra job to pay for this investment."

"And now, how many of these deals at $80 positive cash flow can you afford?" asked rich dad.

I smiled and said, "As many as I can get my hands on."

Rich dad nodded in approval. "Now go out there and get your hands on more of them."

A few years later, the real estate prices in Hawaii did skyrocket. But instead of having only one property go up in value, I had seven double in value. That is the power of a little financial intelligence.

You Can't Do That

When I took my new offer back to the real estate agent, all he said to me was, "You can't do that."

What took the longest time was convincing the agent to start thinking about how we could do what I wanted done. In any event, there were many lessons I learned from this one investment, and one of those lessons was to realize that, when someone says to you, "You can't do that," they may have one finger pointing forward at you, but three fingers are pointing backward at them.

Rich dad taught me that "you can't do that" doesn't necessarily mean you can't. It more often means they can't.

A classic example took place many years ago when people told the Wright brothers, "You can't do that." Thank goodness, the Wright brothers didn't listen.

$1.4 Trillion Looking for a Home

Every day trillions of dollars are moved around the planet electronically. There is more money being created and available today than ever before. The problem is that money is invisible. Today, the bulk of it is electronic. So when people look for money with their eyes, they fail to see anything. Most people struggle to live paycheck to paycheck, and yet $1.4 trillion flies around the world every day looking for someone who wants it. It's looking for someone who knows how to take care of it, nurture it, and grow it. If you know how to take care of money, money will flock to you and be thrown at you. People will beg you to take it.

But if you don't know how to care for money, money will stay away from you. Remember rich dad's definition of financial intelligence: It's not how much money you make, but how much money you keep, how hard it works for you, and how many generations you keep it for.

The Blind Leading the Blind

"The average person is 95 percent eyes and only five percent mind when they invest," said rich dad. "If you want to become a professional in the B and I quadrants, you need to train your eyes to be only five percent and train your mind to see the other 95 percent." Rich dad went on to explain that people who train their minds to see money have tremendous power over people who don't.

He was adamant about whom I took financial advice from. "The reason most people struggle financially is because they take advice from people who are also mentally blind to money. It's the classic tale of the blind leading the blind. If you want money to come to you, you must know how to take care of it. If money isn't first in your head, it won't stick to your hands. If it doesn't stick to your hands, then money, and people with money, will stay away from you."

Train Your Brain to See Money

So what is the first step in training your brain to see money? The answer is easy. It's financial literacy. It begins with the ability to understand the words and the number systems of capitalism. If you don't understand the words or the numbers, you might as well be speaking a foreign language. And, in many cases, each quadrant represents a foreign language.

If you look at the CASHFLOW Quadrant, each quadrant is like a different country. They don't all use the same words, and if you don't understand the words, you won't understand the numbers.

For example, if a medical doctor says, "Your systolic is 120 and your diastolic is 80," is that good or bad? Is that all you need to know for your health? The answer is obviously no, but it's a start.

It's like asking, "My stock's P/E is 12, and my apartment's cap rate is 12. Is this all I need to know for my wealth?" Again, the answer is no, but it's a start. At least we're beginning to speak the same words and use the same numbers. And that is the beginning of financial literacy, which is the basis of financial intelligence. It starts with knowing the words and numbers.

The doctor is speaking from the S quadrant, and the investor is speaking with the words and numbers of the I quadrant. They might as well be speaking different languages.

I disagree when someone says to me, "It takes money to make money." In my opinion, the ability to make money with money begins with understanding the words and the numbers. As my rich dad always said, "If money is not first in your head, it won't stick to your hands."

Know What Real Risk Is

The second step in training your brain to see money is to learn to recognize what real risk is. When people say to me that investing is risky, I simply say, "Investing is not risky. Being uneducated is risky."

Investing is much like flying. If you've been to flight school and spent a number of years gaining experience, then flying is fun and exciting. But if you've never been to flight school, I'd leave the flying to someone else.

Bad Advice Is Risky

Rich dad firmly believed that any financial advice was better than no financial advice. He was a man with an open mind. He was courteous and listened to many people, but he relied ultimately on his own financial intelligence to make his decisions. "If you don't know anything, then any advice is better than no advice. But if you can't tell the difference between bad advice and good advice, then that is risky."

Rich dad firmly believed that most people struggle financially because they operate on financial information handed down from parent to child, and most people don't come from financially sound families. He often said, "Bad financial advice is risky, and most of the bad advice is handed out at home—not from what is said, but from what is done. Children learn by example more than words."

Your Advisors Are Only as Smart as You

Rich dad said, "Your advisors can only be as smart as you are. If you are not smart, they can't tell you that much. If you are financially well-educated, competent advisors can give you more sophisticated financial advice. If you are financially naïve, they must by law offer you only safe and secure financial strategies. If you are an unsophisticated investor, they can only offer low-risk, low-yield investments. They often recommend diversification for unsophisticated investors. Few advisors choose to take the time to teach you, because their time is money. So if you will take it upon yourself to become financially educated and manage your money well, then a competent advisor can inform you about investments and strategies that few will ever see. But first you must do your part to get educated. Always remember, your advisor can only be as smart as you."

Is Your Banker Lying to You?

Rich dad had several bankers he dealt with. They were an important part of his financial team. While he was close friends with and respected his bankers, he always felt he had to watch out for his own best interests, just as he expected the bankers to look out for their own best interests.

After my 1974 investment experience, he asked me this: "When a banker says that your house is an asset, is he telling you the truth?"

Since most people are not financially literate and don't know the game of money, they often must take the opinion and advice of people they tend to trust. If you're not financially literate, then you need to trust someone you hope is. Many people invest or manage their money based on someone else's recommendations more than their own. And that is risky.

They're Not Lying...
They're Just Not Telling You the Whole Truth

The fact is that when a banker says your house is an asset, they're not really lying to you. They're just not telling you the whole truth. While your house is an asset, they simply don't say whose asset it is. If you read financial statements, it's easy to see that your house is not your asset. It is the bank's asset. Remember my rich dad's definitions of an asset and a liability from *Rich Dad Poor Dad:* "An asset puts money in my pocket. A liability takes money out of my pocket."

People on the left side don't really need to know the difference. Most of them are happy to feel secure in their jobs, have a nice house they think they own, are proud of, and think they're in control of. Nobody will take it away from them as long as they make those payments.

But people on the right side need to know the difference. Being financially literate and financially intelligent means being able to understand the big picture of money. Financially astute people know that a mortgage doesn't show up as an asset, but as a liability on your balance sheet. Your mortgage actually shows up as an asset on a balance sheet across town. It shows up as an asset on the bank's balance sheet.

YOUR BALANCE SHEET

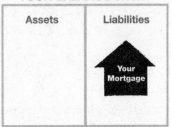

Anyone who has taken accounting knows that a balance sheet must balance. But where does it balance? It doesn't really balance on your balance sheet.

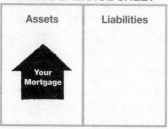

BANK'S BALANCE SHEET

Assets	Liabilities
Your Mortgage	

If you look at the bank's balance sheet, now it balances. Now it makes sense. That is B and I accounting. But this is not the way it's taught in basic accounting. In accounting, you'd show the value of your home as an asset, and the mortgage as a liability. Also, an important point to note is that the value of your home is an opinion that fluctuates with the market, while your mortgage is a definite liability not affected by the market. For a B and I, the value of your home is not considered an asset because it does not generate cash flow.

What Happens if You Pay Off Your Mortgage?

Many people ask me, "What happens if I pay off my mortgage? Is my house an asset then?"

And my reply is, "In most cases, the answer is still no. It's still a liability."

There are several reasons why this is true. One is maintenance and general upkeep. Property is like a car. Even if you own it free and clear, it still costs money to operate, and once things start to break, everything begins to break. In most cases, people pay for repairs on their house and their car with after-tax dollars. A person in the B and I quadrants only includes property as an asset if it generates income through positive cash flow.

But the main reason a house, even without a mortgage, is still a liability is because you still don't own it. The government still taxes you even if you own it. Just stop paying your property taxes, and you'll find out who really owns your property.

That is where tax-lien certificates come from, which I wrote about in *Rich Dad Poor Dad*. Tax-lien certificates are an excellent way to receive up to 16 percent interest on your money. If homeowners don't pay their property taxes, the government charges them interest on the taxes owed, at rates from 10 percent to 50 percent. Talk about being taken to the cleaners! If you don't pay the property taxes, and someone like me pays them for you, then in many states, you owe me the taxes plus the interest. If you don't pay me within a certain amount of time, I get to take your house just for the money I put up. In most states, property taxes take priority in repayment, even before the bank's mortgage. I've had the opportunity to buy houses I paid the taxes on for just a few thousand dollars.

The Definition of Real Estate

Again, to be able to see money, you must see it with your mind, not your eyes. In order to train your mind, you must know the real definitions of words and the system of numbers.

By now, you should know the difference between an asset and a liability, and you should know the definition of the word "mortgage," which is an "agreement until death," and the word "finance," which means "penalty." You will now learn the origin of the words "real estate" and a popular financial vehicle called "derivatives." Many people think derivatives are new, but in reality, they're ages old.

A simple definition of derivative is "something that comes from something else." An example of a derivative is orange juice. Orange juice is a derivative of an orange.

I used to think that real estate meant "real" or something that was tangible. My rich dad explained to me that it really comes from the Spanish word real, which means "royal." El camino real means the royal road. Real estate means the royal estate.

Once the Agrarian Age came to an end and the Industrial Age began around 1500, power was no longer based on the land and agriculture. The monarchs realized they had to change in response to the land-reform acts that allowed peasants to own the land. So royalty created derivatives, such as taxes on land ownership and mortgages, as a way of allowing commoners to finance their land. Taxes and mortgages are derivatives because they are derived from the land. Your banker would not call the mortgage a derivative. They would say it is secured by the land—different words, similar meanings. So once royalty realized that money was no longer in the land, but in the derivatives that came from the land, the monarchs set up banks to handle the increased business. Today, land is still called real estate because, no matter how much you pay for it, it never really belongs to you. It still belongs to the royals.

What Is Your Interest Rate... Really?

Rich dad fought and negotiated tough for every single point of interest he paid. He asked me this question: "When a banker tells you your interest rate is eight percent per annum, is it really?" I found out it's not if you learn to read numbers.

Let's say you buy a $100,000 home, make a down payment of $20,000 and borrow the remaining $80,000 at eight percent interest with a 30-year term from your bank.

In five years you will pay a total of $35,220 to the bank: $31,276 for interest, and only $3,944 for debt reduction.

If you take the loan to term, or 30 years, you will have paid $211,323 total principal and interest, less what you originally borrowed—$80,000. The total interest you will have paid: $131,323.

By the way, that $211,323 doesn't include property taxes and insurance on the loan.

Funny, $131,323 seems to be a little bit more than eight percent of $80,000. It's more like 160 percent in interest over 30 years. As I said, they're not lying. They're just not telling the whole truth. And if you can't read numbers, you'd really never know. And if you're happy with your house, you'll never really care.

But, of course, the industry knows that in a few years you're going to want a new house, a bigger house, a smaller house, a vacation house, or a refinance on your mortgage. They know it and, in fact, they count on it.

Industry Average

In the banking industry, a seven-year average is used as the life expectancy for a mortgage. That means banks expect the average person to buy a new house or refinance every seven years. And that means, in this example, they expect to get their original $80,000 back every seven years, plus $43,291 in interest.

And that's why it is called a mortgage, which comes from the French word "mortir" or "agreement until death." The reality is that most people will continue to work hard, get pay raises, and buy new houses with new mortgages. On top of that, the government gives a tax break to encourage taxpayers to buy more expensive houses, which means higher property taxes for the government.

Every time I watch television, I see commercials where handsome athletes smile and tell you to take all your credit-card debt and roll it into a bill-consolidation loan. That way, you can pay off those credit cards and carry a new loan at a lower interest rate. They tell you why it's financially intelligent to do this: "A bill-consolidation loan is a smart move on your part because the government gives you a tax deduction for the interest payments you make on your home mortgage."

Viewers, thinking they see the light, run down to their finance company, refinance their home, pay off their credit cards, and feel intelligent.

A few weeks later, they're shopping and see a new dress, a new lawn mower, or realize their kid needs a new bicycle or they need to take a vacation because they're exhausted. They have excellent credit, they pay their bills, their little heart goes pitter-patter, and they say to themselves, "Oh, go on. You deserve it. You can pay it off a little every month."

Emotions overpower logic, and the credit card comes out of hiding. As I said, when bankers say your house is an asset, they are not lying. When the government gives you a tax break for being in debt, it is not because they're concerned about your financial future. The government is concerned about its financial future. So when your banker, your accountant, your attorney, and your teachers tell you that your house is an asset, they just fail to say whose asset it is.

What About Savings? Are They Assets?

Now, your savings really are assets. That's the good news. But again, if you read financial statements, you'll understand the total picture. While it's true that your savings are assets, when you look across town at the bank's balance sheet, your savings show up as a liability.

This is what your savings and checkbook balance look like in your asset column:

YOUR BALANCE SHEET

Assets	Liabilities
Your Savings	
Your Checkbook Balance	

And this is how your savings and your checkbook balance are carried on your bank's balance sheet:

BANK'S BALANCE SHEET

Assets	Liabilities
	Your Savings
	Your Checkbook Balance

Why are your savings and checkbook balances a liability to banks? Because they have to pay you interest for your money, and it costs them money to safeguard it.

If you can grasp the significance of these few drawings and words, you might begin to better understand what the eyes cannot see about the game of money.

Why You Don't Get a Tax Break for Saving Money

If you notice, you get a tax break for buying a house and going into debt, but you don't get a tax break for saving money. Have you ever wondered why?

I'm not sure either, but I imagine that one big reason is because your savings are a liability to banks. Why would they ask the government to pass a law that would encourage you to put even more money in their bank, money that is a liability to them?

They Don't Need Your Savings

Besides, banks really don't need your savings. They don't need much in deposits because they can magnify money at least 10 times. If you put $1 in the bank, by law, the bank can lend out $10 and, depending upon the reserve limits imposed by the central bank, possibly much more. That means your single $1 suddenly becomes $10 or more. It's magic! When my rich dad showed me that, I fell in love with the idea. At that point, I knew that I wanted to own a bank and not go to school to become a banker.

On top of that, the bank may pay less than one percent interest on that one dollar. In better economic times, it could be five percent and you, as a consumer, would feel secure because the bank is paying you something on your money. Banks see this as good customer relations because, if you have savings with them, you may come in and borrow money too. They want you to do this because they can then charge nine percent or more on what you borrow. While you may make less than one percent on your $1, the bank can make nine percent or more on the $10 of debt your single dollar has generated. Recently, I received a new credit-card offer that advertised 8.9 percent interest. But since I understood the legal jargon in the fine print, I saw it was really 23 percent. Needless to say, I took a pass.

They Get Your Savings Anyway

The other reason they don't offer a tax break for savings is more obvious. If you can read the numbers and see which way the cash is flowing, you'll notice that they'll get your savings anyway. The money you could be saving in your asset column is flowing instead out of your liability column in the form of interest payments on your mortgage. This ends up in the bank's asset column. The cash-flow pattern looks like this:

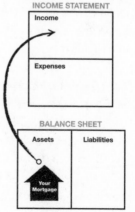

YOUR FINANCIAL STATEMENT   YOUR BANK'S FINANCIAL STATEMENT

INCOME STATEMENT

Income

Expenses

Your Mortgage Interest

BALANCE SHEET

Assets   Liabilities

Your Mortgage

INCOME STATEMENT

Income

Expenses

BALANCE SHEET

Assets   Liabilities

Your Mortgage

That's why they don't need the government to give you a tax incentive to save. They'll get your savings anyway in the form of interest payments on debt.

Politicians aren't about to mess with the system because the banks, insurance companies, building industry, brokerage houses, and others contribute a lot of money to their campaigns, and the politicians know the name of the game.

The Name of the Game

In 1974 my rich dad was upset because the game was played against me, and I didn't know it. I had bought this investment property and had taken a losing position, yet I'd been led to believe it was a winning position.

"I'm glad you entered the game," said rich dad. "But because no one has ever told you what the game is, you've just been suckered over to the losing team."

Rich dad then explained the basics of the game. "The name of the game of capitalism is: 'Who Is Indebted to Whom?'" Once I knew the game, I could be a better player instead of someone who just had the game run all over them.

The More People You Are Indebted to, the Poorer You Are

"The more people you're indebted to, the poorer you are," said rich dad. "And the more people you have indebted to you, the wealthier you are. That's the game."

As I said, I struggled to keep my mind open. So I stayed silent and let him explain.

"We're all in debt to someone else. The problems occur when the debt gets out of balance. Unfortunately, the poor people of this world have been run over so hard by the game that they often can't get any deeper into debt. The same is true for poor countries. The world simply takes from the poor, the weak, and the financially uninformed. If you have too much debt, the world takes everything you have, including your time, your work, your home, your life, your confidence— even your dignity, if you let them. I don't make the rules, but I do know the game, and I play it well. I'll explain the game to you if you want to learn to play. Then, after you've mastered the game, you can decide what to do with what you know."

Money Is Debt

Rich dad went on to explain that even our currency isn't an instrument of equity, but an instrument of debt. Every dollar used to be backed by gold or silver but is now an IOU guaranteed to be paid by the taxpayers of the issuing country. As long as the rest of the world has confidence in the American taxpayer to work and pay for this IOU called money, the world has confidence in our dollar. If that key element of money, confidence, suddenly disappears, the economy comes down like a house of cards.

Take the example of the German Weimar-government marks that became utterly worthless just before World War II. As one story goes, an elderly woman was pushing a wheelbarrow full of marks to buy a loaf of bread. When she turned her back, someone stole the wheelbarrow and left the pile of worthless money all over the street.

That's why most money today is known as "fiat" money, money that cannot be converted to something tangible like gold or silver. The money is only good as long as people have confidence in the government backing it.

Today, much of the global economy is based on debt and confidence. As long as we all keep holding hands and no one breaks ranks, everything will be fine. By the way, the word "fine" is my acronym for "Feeling Insecure, Neurotic and Emotional."

Who Is Indebted to Whom?

Going back to 1974 when I was learning how to buy that $56,000 condo, my rich dad taught me an important lesson on how to structure deals.

"'Who Is Indebted to Whom' is the name of the game," said rich dad. "And somebody just stuck you with the debt. It's like going to dinner with ten friends. You go to the restroom and when you come back, the bill is there, but all ten friends are gone. If you're going to play the game, then you had better understand it, know the rules, speak the same language, and know with whom you're playing. If you don't, instead of playing the game, the game will be played on you."

It's Only a Game

At first I got angry at what rich dad was saying, but I listened and did my best to understand. Finally, he put it into a context that I could understand. "You love playing football, don't you?" he asked.

I nodded my head. "I love the game," I said.

"Well, money is my game," said rich dad. "I love the money game."

"But for many people, money isn't a game," I said.

"That's correct," said rich dad. "For most people, it's survival. For most people, money is a game they're forced to play, and they hate it. Unfortunately, the more civilized we get, the more money becomes a part of our lives."

Rich dad drew the CASHFLOW Quadrant.

"Just look at this as a tennis court, football field, or soccer field. If you're going to play the money game, which team do you want to be on: the E's, S's, B's, or I's? Or which side of the court do you want to be on: the right side or the left?"

I quickly pointed to the right side.

If You Take on Debt and Risk, You Should Be Paid

"Good," said rich dad. "That's why you can't go out there to play the game and believe some sales agent when he tells you that to lose $150 a month for 30 years is a good deal because the government will give you a tax break for losing money and he expects the price of real estate to go up. You simply can't play the game with that mindset. While those opinions might come true, that's just not the way the game is played on the right side of the CASHFLOW Quadrant. Somebody is telling you to go into debt, take all the risks, and pay for it. People on the left side think that's a good idea, but not the people on the right."

I was shaking a little. "Look at it my way," said rich dad. "You're willing to pay $56,000 for this condo in the sky. You're signing for the debt and taking all the risk. The tenant pays less in rent than what it costs to live there. So you're subsidizing that person's housing. Does that make sense to you?"

I shook my head.

"This is the way I play the game," said rich dad. "From now on, if you take on debt and risk, then you should get paid. Got that?"

I nodded my head.

"Making money is common sense," said rich dad. "It's not rocket science. But unfortunately, when it comes to money, common sense is uncommon. A banker tells you to take on debt so the government can give you a tax break. That doesn't make fundamental economic sense. Then a real estate agent tells you to sign the papers because he can find a tenant who will pay you less than you're paying but, in his opinion, the value of the condo will go up. If that makes sense to you, then you and I don't share the same common sense."

I just stood there. I heard everything he said, and I had to admit that I'd gotten so excited by what I thought looked like a good deal that my logic went out the window and I didn't analyze the deal. Because the deal looked good, I had become emotional with greed and excitement, and I was no longer able to hear what the numbers and the words were telling me.

It was then that rich dad gave me an important rule that he has always used, "Your profit is made when you buy, not when you sell."

Rich dad had to be certain that whatever debt or risk he took on, it made sense from the day he bought it. It had to make sense if the economy got worse, and it had to make sense if the economy got better. He never bought on tax tricks or crystal-ball forecasts of the future. A deal had to make sound economic sense in good times and in bad.

I was beginning to understand the game of money as he saw it. Clearly, the game was to see others become indebted to you, and to be careful to whom you became indebted. Today, I still hear his words: "If you take on risk and debt, make sure you get paid for it."

Rich dad had debt, but he was careful when he took it on. "If you take on debt personally, make sure it's small. If you take on large debt, make sure someone else is paying for it."

He saw the game of money and debt as a game that is played on you, played on me, played on everyone. It's played from business to business, and it's played from country to country. To him it was only a game. But for most people, money isn't a game. It's survival. And because no one explained the game to them, they still believe bankers who say a house is an asset.

The Importance of Facts versus Opinions

Rich dad continued his lesson: "If you want to be successful on the right side, you've got to know the difference between facts and opinions. You can't blindly accept financial advice the way people on the left side do. You must know the numbers. The numbers will tell you the facts. Your financial survival depends upon facts, not some friend or advisor's wordy opinions."

"I don't understand. What's the big deal about something being a fact or an opinion? Is one better than the other?"

"No," replied rich dad. "Just know when something is a fact and when something is an opinion."

Still puzzled, I stood there with a confused look on my face.

"What is your family's home worth?" asked rich dad.

"Oh, I know," I replied quickly. "My parents are thinking about selling so they had a real estate agent come in and do an appraisal. They said the house was worth $36,000. That means my dad's net worth increased by $16,000 because he only paid $20,000 for it five years ago."

"So is the appraisal and your dad's net worth a fact or an opinion?" asked rich dad.

I thought about it for a while and understood what he was getting at. "Both are opinions, aren't they?"

Rich dad nodded his head. "Very good. Most people struggle financially because they spend their lives using opinions rather than facts when making financial decisions—opinions such as:

- "Your house is an asset."

- "The price of real estate always goes up."

- "Blue-chip stocks are your best investment."

- "It takes money to make money."

- "Stocks have always outperformed real estate."

- "You should diversify your portfolio."

- "You have to be dishonest to be rich."

- "Investing is risky."

- "Play it safe."

I sat there deep in thought, realizing that most of what I heard about money at home was really people's opinions, not facts.

"Is gold an asset?" asked rich dad, snapping me out of my daydream.

"Yes. Of course," I replied. "It's the only real money that has withstood the test of time."

"See, there you go again," smiled rich dad. "All you're doing is repeating someone else's opinion about what is an asset rather than checking out the facts."

"Gold is only an asset, by my definition, if you buy it for less than you sell it for," rich dad said slowly. "In other words, if you bought it for $100 and sold it for $200, then it was an asset. But if you bought one ounce for $200 and you sold it for $100, then gold in this transaction was a liability. It is the actual financial numbers of the transaction that ultimately tell you the facts. In reality, the only thing that is an asset or liability is you, because only you can make decisions that make gold an asset or a liability. That is why financial education is so important. I've seen so many people take a perfectly good business or piece of real estate and turn it into a financial nightmare. Many people do the same in their personal lives. They take hard-earned money and create a lifetime of financial liabilities."

I was even more confused, a little hurt inside, and wanted to argue. Rich dad was toying with my brain.

"Many a man has been suckered because he didn't know the facts. Every day I hear horror stories of someone who lost all their money because they thought an opinion was a fact. It's okay to use an opinion when making a financial decision, but you must know the difference. Millions of people have made life decisions based upon opinions handed down from generation to generation. And then they wonder why they struggle financially."

"What kind of opinions?" I asked.

Rich dad chuckled to himself before he answered, "Well, let me give you a few common ones we have all heard."

- "You should marry him. He'll make a good husband."

- "Find a secure job and stay there all your life."

- "Doctors make a lot of money."

- "They have a big house. They must be rich."

- "He has big muscles. He must be healthy."

- "This is a nice car. It's only been driven by a little old lady."

- "There is not enough money for everyone to be rich."

- "The earth is flat."

- "Humans will never fly."

- "He's smarter than his sister."

- "Bonds are safer than stocks."

- "People who make mistakes are stupid."

- "He will never sell for such a low price."

- "She will never go out with me."

- "Investing is risky."

- "I'll never be rich."

- "I didn't go to college so I'll never get ahead."

- "You should diversify your investments."

- "You should not diversify your investments."

Rich dad went on and on until finally he could tell I was tired of hearing his examples of opinions.

"Okay! I've heard enough. What's your point?"

"Thought you'd never stop me," rich dad said, smiling. "The point is that most people's lives are determined by their opinions, rather than the facts. For a person's life to change, they first need to change their opinions and then start looking at the facts. If you can read financial statements, you'll be able to see the facts of an individual's or a company's financial success rather than going by opinions—yours or somebody else's. As I said, one is not better than the other. But, to be successful in life, especially financially, you must know the difference. If you can't verify something is a fact, then it's an opinion. Financial blindness occurs when a person can't read a financial statement, leaving them to rely on someone else's opinion. Financial insanity is caused when opinions are used as facts. If you want to be on the right side of the CASHFLOW Quadrant, you must know the difference between facts and opinions. Few lessons are more important than this one."

I sat there listening quietly, doing my best to understand what he was saying. It was obviously a simple concept, yet it was larger than my brain could accept at that moment.

"Do you know what due diligence is?" rich dad asked.

I shook my head.

Due diligence simply means doing your homework and finding out which statements are opinions and which are facts. When it comes to money, most people are either lazy or searching for shortcuts, so they don't do enough due diligence. And there are still others who are so afraid of making mistakes that all they do is due diligence and then do nothing. Too much due diligence is also called 'analysis paralysis.' The point is that you must know how to sift through facts and opinions, and then make your decision. As I said, most people are in financial trouble today simply because they've taken too many shortcuts and are making their life's financial decisions based upon opinions (often the opinions of an E or an S) and not the facts. If you want to be a B or an I, you must be keenly aware of this difference."

I didn't fully appreciate rich dad's lesson that day, yet few lessons have served me better than that one.

Years later, in the early 1990s, rich dad watched the stock market climb out of sight. His only comment was: "That's what happens when highly paid employees or self-employed people with big pay checks, paying excessive amounts in taxes, greatly in debt, and with only paper assets in their portfolio begin handing out investment advice. Millions are about to get hurt following the opinions of people who think they know the facts."

Warren Buffett, America's greatest investor, once said, "If you're in a poker game and after 20 minutes you don't know who the patsy is, then you're the patsy."

Why People Struggle Financially

Would you believe that most people will be in debt from the day they leave school until the day they die? It's true. This is the average middle-class American's financial picture:

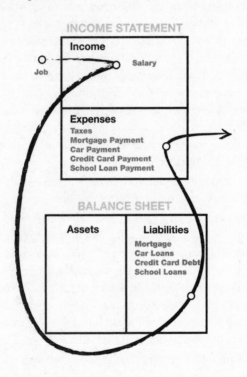

Someone Else's Balance Sheet

If you now understand the game, then you may realize that those liabilities must show up on someone else's balance sheet as assets, like this:

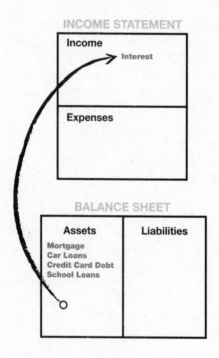

Anytime you hear these words, "Low down payment. Easy monthly payments," or "Don't worry. The government will give you a tax break for those losses," then you know someone is luring you into the game. If you want to be financially free, you've got to be smarter than that.

Most people don't have anyone who is indebted to them. They have no real assets (things that put money in their pocket), and they're often indebted to everyone else. That's why they cling to job security and struggle financially. If it weren't for their job, they'd be broke in a flash. In fact, the average American is less than three paychecks away from bankruptcy. They seek a better life and get run over by the game because the deck is stacked against them. They still think their house, car, golf clubs, clothes, vacation home, and other doodads are assets. They believe what someone else tells them because they can't read financial numbers to see the truth for themselves. Most people go to school and learn to be players in the game, but no one explains the rules to them. No one tells them that the name of the game is: "Who Is Indebted to Whom?" And because no one tells them that, they are the ones who become indebted to everyone else.

Money Is an Idea

I hope you now understand the basics of the CASHFLOW Quadrant and know that money really is an idea that is more clearly seen with your mind than with your eyes. Learning the game of money and how it is played is an important part of your journey to financial freedom. Even more important is who you need to become to move to the right side of the CASHFLOW Quadrant. Part II of this book focuses on "Bringing Out the Best in You" and on analyzing the formula:

Be

Do

Have

Part Two

BRINGING OUT
THE BEST IN YOU

Chapter Seven
BECOMING WHO YOU ARE

*The real issue is the changes you must go through
and who you become in the process.*

"It's not being homeless that matters," my rich dad said. "It's about who you are. Keep striving and you'll become somebody. Quit, and you'll also become somebody, but not the same person."

The Changes You Go Through

For those of you contemplating going from job security to financial security, all I can offer you are words of encouragement. For Kim and me, it took being homeless and desperate before I found the courage to move forward. That was our path, but it definitely doesn't have to be your path. As I described earlier, there are ready-made systems that can help you cross the bridge to the right side of the CASHFLOW Quadrant.

The real issue is the changes you must go through internally and who you become in the process. For some people, the process is easy. For others, the journey is impossible.

Money Is a Drug

Rich dad always said to Mike and me, "Money is a drug." The main reason he refused to pay us while we worked for him was because he never wanted us to become addicted to working for money. "If you become addicted to money, it's hard to break that addiction."

When I called him from California as a grown man to ask him for money, he wasn't about to break a pattern he started with me years before. He didn't give us money as kids, and he wasn't about to start now. Instead, he continued to be tough and guide me away from the addiction of working for money.

He called money a drug because he observed people who were happy when they had money and upset or moody when they didn't. Just as heroin addicts get high when they inject the drug, they also get moody and violent when they don't have it.

"Be careful of money's addictive power," he often said. "Once you get used to receiving it, that addiction keeps you attached to the way you got it."

Put another way, if you receive money as an employee, then you get accustomed to that way of acquiring it. If you get used to generating money by being self-employed, it's often difficult to break the attachment to earning money in that way. And if you get used to government handouts, that, too, is a hard pattern to break.

"The hardest part about moving from the left side to the right side is the attachment you have to the way you are used to earning money," said rich dad. "It's more than breaking a habit. It's breaking an addiction."

That's why he stressed to Mike and me to never work for money. He insisted we learn to create our own systems as a way of acquiring money.

The Patterns

For Kim and me, the hardest part in trying to become people who generate income in the B and I quadrants was that all of our past conditioning was holding us back. It was tough when friends said, "Why are you doing this? Why don't you just get a job?"

It was even more difficult because there was a part of us that also wanted to go back to the security of a paycheck.

Rich dad explained to Mike and me that the world of money was one large system. And we as individuals learn how to operate in certain patterns within that system.

An E works for the system.
An S is the system.
A B creates, owns, and/or controls the system.
An I invests money into the system.

The pattern rich dad was talking about was the pattern we naturally gravitate to when it comes to money.

"When a person feels the need for money," rich dad explained, "an E will automatically look for a job, an S often will do something alone, a B will create or buy a system that produces money, and an I will look for an opportunity to invest in an asset that produces more money."

Why It's Hard to Change a Pattern

"The reason it's hard to change a pattern is because money today is essential for life. In the Agrarian Age, money wasn't that important because the land could provide food, shelter, warmth, and water without money. Once we moved into cities during the Industrial Age, money signified life itself. Today, even water costs money," said rich dad.

He went on to explain that when you begin to move from, let's say, the E quadrant to the B quadrant, the part of you that is addicted to being an E or afraid that life will end, begins to kick and fight back. It's like a drowning person beginning to fight for air. Or a starving man who will eat anything to survive.

"It's this internal battle that makes it so hard. The struggle between who you no longer are and who you want to become is the problem," rich dad explained to me over the phone. "The part of you that still seeks security is in a war with that part of you that wants freedom. Only you can decide which will win. You will either build that business, or you'll go back to finding a job—forever."

Find Your Passion

"Do you really want to move forward?" asked rich dad.

"Yes!" I said hurriedly.

"Have you forgotten what you set out to do? Have you forgotten about your passion and what caused you to get into this predicament in the first place?" asked rich dad.

"Oh," I replied, a little startled. I had forgotten. I stood there at the pay phone, clearing my head so I could remember what got me into this mess in the first place.

"I knew it," said rich dad, his voice booming over the phone. "You're more worried about your own personal survival than keeping your dream alive. Your fear has pushed aside your passion. The best way to keep going is to keep the flame in your heart alive. Always remember what you set out to do, and the trip will be easy. Start worrying more about yourself, and your fear begins to eat away at your soul. Passion builds businesses, not fear. You've come this far. You're close, so don't turn back now. Remember what you set out to do, keep that memory in your heart and keep the flame going. You can always quit. So why quit now?"

With that, rich dad wished me luck and hung up the phone. He was correct. I had forgotten why I set out on this journey. I had lost my dream and allowed my fears to fill my head as well as my heart. I had forgotten my passion. It was now time to make it happen or go back home and forget about it. I stood

there for a while, and again I heard rich dad's last words: "You can always quit. So why quit now?"
I decided to delay quitting until I made things happen.

Becoming a Teacher Who Owned the System

My fears and lack of success were beating me, and my dream had been pushed aside. My dream was to create a different kind of school system—an educational program for people who want to become entrepreneurs and investors. As I stood there, my mind drifted back to high school.

When I was 15, my high school guidance counselor asked me, "What are you going to do when you grow up? Are you going to become a teacher like your dad?"

Looking straight at my counselor, my answer was straightforward, strong, and filled with conviction. "I'll never be a teacher. Becoming a teacher is the last thing I would ever do."

I didn't just dislike school—I hated it. I absolutely hated being forced to sit and listen to someone I didn't particularly like or respect speak for months on a subject I had no interest in. I fidgeted, squirmed, caused problems in the back of the room, or simply skipped class.

So when my guidance counselor asked me if I was planning to seek a career as a teacher following in my father's footsteps, I nearly jumped out of my skin.

Little did I know at the time that passion is a combination of love and hate. I loved learning, but I hated school. I absolutely detested sitting there and being programmed into becoming something I did not want to be. I was not alone.

Notable Quotes on Education

Winston Churchill once said: "Personally, I am always ready to learn, although I do not always like being taught."

John Updike said: "The founding fathers, in their wisdom, decided that children were an unnatural strain on their parents. So they provided jails called school, equipped with tortures called education."

Norman Douglas said: "Education is the state-controlled manufacture of echoes."

H.L. Mencken said: "School days, I believe, are the unhappiest in the whole span of human existence. They are full of dull, unintelligible tasks, new and unpleasant ordinances, and brutal violations of common sense and common decency."

Galileo said: "You cannot teach a person anything. You can only help him find it within himself."

Mark Twain said: "I never let schooling interfere with my education."

Albert Einstein said: "There is too much education altogether, especially in American schools."

A Gift from My Educated Dad

The person who shared these quotes with me was my highly educated, but poor, dad. He also despised the school system, although he thrived in it. He became a teacher because he also dreamed of changing the system, but instead the system crushed him. He took his passion, tried to change the system, and ran into a brick wall. It was a system that too many people were making money in, and no one wanted it changed, although there was a lot of talk about the need for change.

Maybe my guidance counselor was psychic, because years later I did indeed follow in my father's footsteps. I just didn't follow him into the same system. I was taking that same passion and creating my own system.

When my educated dad learned that Kim and I were struggling financially, doing our best to set up our own educational system, he sent us those quotes. Scribbled across the top of the page of the quotes were these words: "Keep going. Love, Dad."

Up until that moment, I never knew how much my educated dad hated the system and what it did to young people. But after this gesture of encouragement, things began to make sense. The passion that was driving me then was the same passion that had driven him years earlier. I was just like my real dad, and I'd unwittingly picked up the torch from him. I was a teacher at the core. Maybe that's why I hated the system so much.

In hindsight, I had become both dads. From my rich dad, I learned the secrets of being a capitalist. From my highly educated dad, I inherited the passion for teaching. With this combination, I could now do something about the educational system. I didn't have the desire or ability to change the current system, but I did have the knowledge to create my own system.

The Years of Training Begin to Pay Off

For years, my rich dad groomed me to become a person who created businesses and business systems. The business I set up in 1977 was a manufacturing company. We were one of the first companies to produce the nylon-and-Velcro surfer wallets that came in bright colors. We followed that product with "the shoe pocket"—a miniature wallet, also made of nylon and Velcro, that attached to the shoe laces of running shoes. In 1978, jogging was the new craze, and runners always wanted a place to put their keys, money, and ID cards.

Our meteoric success was phenomenal, but soon the passion for the product line and the business drifted away. It began to weaken once my little company was pounded by foreign competition. Taiwan, South Korea, and Hong Kong were shipping products identical to mine and wiping out the markets we developed. Their prices were so low that there was no way we could compete. They were retailing products for less than it cost us to manufacture them.

Our little company was faced with a dilemma: Fight them, or join them. My partners and I realized we couldn't win the battle. The companies flooding the market with cheap products were too strong. A vote was taken, and we decided to join them.

The tragedy was that, in order to stay afloat, we had to let go of most of our faithful and hardworking staff. That broke my heart.

When I inspected the new factories we contracted with for our manufacturing in Korea and Taiwan, my soul died a little. The working conditions these young workers were forced into were cruel and inhumane. I saw five workers stacked one on top of the other in a space where we would only allow one worker. My conscience began to bother me deeply, not only for the workers we let go in America, but also for our new workers overseas.

Although we had solved the financial problem of foreign competition and began to make a lot of money, my heart was no longer in the business. Consequently, the business began to suffer. Its spirit was gone because my spirit was gone. I no longer wanted to become rich if it meant exploiting so many low-paid workers. I began to think about educating people to become owners of businesses rather than employees of business. At age 32, I was beginning to become a teacher, but I didn't realize it at the time. The business began to decline, not due to a lack of systems, but because of a lack of heart or passion. By the time Kim and I started out on our new business venture, the wallet company was gone.

Downsizing Coming

In 1983, I was invited to give a talk to the MBA class at the University of Hawaii. I gave them my views on job security. They didn't like what I had to say: "In a few years, many of you will lose your jobs, or be forced to work for less and less money, with less and less security."

Because my work caused me to travel the world, I witnessed firsthand the combined power of cheap labor and innovations from technology. I realized that a worker in Asia, Europe, Russia, or South America was really competing with workers in America. I knew the idea of high pay and a safe, secure job for workers and middle managers was an idea whose time had passed. Big companies would soon have to make cuts, both in their number of employees and in the dollars they paid to workers, simply to be able to compete globally.

I was never asked back to the University of Hawaii. A few years later, the word "downsizing" became commonplace. Every time a big company merged with another company, workers became redundant and downsizing occurred. Every time the owners wanted to make their shareholders happy, a downsizing occurred. With each downsizing, I saw the people at the top get richer and richer, and the people at the bottom pay the price.

Every time I heard someone say, "I'm sending my child to a good school so he or she can get a good, safe, secure job," I cringed. Being prepared for a job is a good idea for the short term, but it is not enough for the long term. Slowly but surely, I was becoming a teacher.

Build a System Around Your Passion

Although my manufacturing company had turned around and was doing well again, my passion was gone. Rich dad summed up my frustration when he said, "School days are over. It's time to build a system around your heart. Build a system around your passion. Let the manufacturing company go, and build what you know you must build. You've learned well from me, but you're still your father's son. You and your dad are teachers deep in your souls."

Kim and I packed up everything and moved to California to learn new teaching methods so we could create a business around those methods. Before we could get the business off the ground, we ran out of money and were out on the street. It was that phone call to my rich dad, my wife standing by me, anger at myself, and a rekindling of the passion that got us out of the mess we were in.

Soon we were back to building a company. The company was an educational company using teaching methods that were almost the exact opposite of those used in traditional schools. Instead of asking students to sit still, we encouraged them to be active. Instead of teaching via lecture, we taught by playing games. Instead of being boring, we insisted our teachers be fun. Instead of teachers, we sought out business people who actually started their own companies and could teach using our style of teaching. Instead of grading the students, the students graded the teacher. If the teacher got a lousy grade, the teacher was either put through another intensive training program or asked to leave.

Age, educational background, sex, and religious beliefs were not criteria. All we asked for was a sincere desire to learn, and to learn quickly. We were eventually able to teach a year's worth of accounting in one day.

Although we mainly taught adults, we had many teenagers learning right alongside highly paid, well-educated business executives. Instead of competing on tests, we asked them to cooperate on teams. Then we had the team take a test, competing against other teams taking the same test. Instead of striving for grades, we bet money—with winner take all. The competition and desire to do well as a team was fierce. The teacher did not have to motivate the class. He or she just had to get out of the way once the learning competition began. Instead of quiet at test time, there was yelling, screaming, laughter and tears. People were excited about learning. They were turned on by learning, and they wanted to learn more.

We focused on teaching just two subjects: entrepreneurship and investing, the B and I quadrants. The people who wanted to learn these subjects in our style of education showed up in droves. We did not advertise. Everything spread by word of mouth. The people who showed up were people who wanted to create jobs, not look for jobs.

Once I made up my mind not to quit that night at the phone booth, things began to move forward. In less than five years, we had a multimillion-dollar business with 11 offices throughout the world. We had built a new system of education, and the market loved it. Our passion had made it happen, because passion and a good system overcame fear and past programming.

A Teacher Can Be Rich

Whenever I hear teachers say they aren't paid enough, I feel for them. The irony is that they are a product of their own system's programming. They look at being a teacher from the point of view of the E quadrant rather than the B or I quadrant. Remember, you can be anything you want to be in any of the quadrants, even a teacher.

We Can Be Anything We Want

Most of us have the potential to be successful in all of the quadrants. It all depends on how determined we are to be successful. As my rich dad said, "Passion builds businesses—not fear."

The problem of changing quadrants is often found in our past conditioning. Many of us came from families where the emotion of fear was used as a prime motivator to get us to think and act in a certain way. For example: "Did you do your homework? If you don't do your homework, you'll flunk out of school and all your friends will laugh at you." "If you keep making faces, your face will get stuck in that position." And the classic, "If you don't get good grades, you won't get a safe, secure job with benefits."

Well, today many people have gotten good grades, but there are fewer safe, secure jobs, and even fewer with benefits like pensions. Many people, even those with good grades, need to "mind their own business" and not just look for a job where they will mind someone else's business.

It's Risky on the Left Side

I have many friends who still seek security through a job. Ironically, the march of technology continues at an ever-increasing pace. To keep up in the job market, each person will need to constantly be trained in the latest technology. If you're going to be reeducated anyway, why not spend some time educating yourself on the skills needed for the right side of the CASHFLOW Quadrant? If people could see what I see when I travel the world, they would not be looking for more security. Security is a myth. Learn something new, and take on this brave new world. Don't hide from it.

It is also risky for self-employed people. If they get sick or injured, their income is directly impacted. As I get older, I meet more self-employed people my age who are physically, mentally, and emotionally burned out from hard work. The more fatigue a person endures, the less secure they become, and the risk of them having an accident also goes up.

It Is More Secure on the Right Side

The irony is that life is actually more secure on the right side of the CASHFLOW Quadrant. For example, if you have a secure system that produces more and more money with less and less work, then you really don't need a job or need to worry about losing your job. To make more money, simply expand the system and hire more people. I apply the same principle when I teach about expanding your means rather than living below your means. Living below your means crushes the spirit, and I have always looked for ways to expand my means so that I can enjoy all that life has to offer.

People who are high-level investors aren't concerned about the market going up or down because their knowledge allows them to make money either way. If there is a market crash and/or a depression in the next 30 years, many baby boomers will panic and lose much of the money they had set aside for retirement. If that happens in their old age, instead of retiring, they'll have to work for as long as they can.

Professional investors are people who risk little of their own money and yet still make the highest returns. The people who know little about investing take the risks and earn the least return. From my point of view, all the risk is on the left side of the CASHFLOW Quadrant.

Why the Left Side Is Riskier

"If you can't read numbers, then you must take someone else's opinion," said rich dad. "In the case of buying a house, your dad just blindly accepts your banker's opinion that his house is an asset."

Both Mike and I noticed his emphasis on the word "blindly."

"Most people on the left side really do not need to be that good with financial numbers. But if you want to be successful on the right side, then numbers become your eyes. Numbers allow you to see what most people don't see," rich dad went on.

"You mean like Superman's X-ray vision?" asked Mike.

Rich dad chuckled and nodded. "Exactly," he said. "The ability to read numbers, financial systems, and business systems gives you vision that mere mortals don't have." Even he laughed at that silliness.

"Having financial vision lowers your risk. Being financially blind increases risk. But you only need that vision if you want to operate on the right side. People on the left side think in words. To be successful on the right side, especially the I quadrant, you must think in numbers. It's very risky trying to be an investor while still thinking predominantly in words."

"Are you saying that people on the left side don't need to know anything about financial numbers?" I asked.

"For most of them, that's correct," said rich dad. "As long as they're content to operate strictly within the confines of being an E or an S, then the numbers they learn in school are adequate. But if they want to survive on the right side, understanding financial numbers and systems becomes crucial. If you want to build a small business, you don't need to master numbers. But if you want build a large worldwide business, numbers become everything, not words. That is why so many large companies are often run by bean-counters."

Rich dad continued his lesson, "If you want to be successful on the right side, when it comes to money, you must know the difference between facts and opinions. You cannot blindly accept financial advice the way people on the left side do. You must know your numbers. You must know the facts. And numbers tell you the facts."

Who Pays to Take the Risk?

"Besides the left side being risky, people on that side pay to take that risk," said rich dad.

"What do you mean?" I asked. "Doesn't everyone pay to take risks?"

"No," said rich dad. "Not on the right side."

"Are you trying to say that people on the left side pay to take risks, and people on the right side get paid to take risks?"

"That's exactly what I mean," said rich dad, smiling. "That is the biggest difference between the left side and the right side. That is why the left side is riskier than the right."

"Can you give me an example?" I asked.

"Sure," said rich dad. "If you buy shares of stock in a company, who takes the financial risk? You, or the company?"

"I guess I do," I said, still puzzled.

"And if I'm a medical insurance company and I insure your health and take on your health risk, do I pay you?"

"No," I said. "If they insure my health and they take that risk, I pay for it."

"That's right," said rich dad. "I have yet to find an insurance company that will insure your health or accident risk and pay you for that privilege. But that's what people on the left side do."

"It's kind of confusing," said Mike. "It still doesn't make sense."

Rich dad smiled, "Once you better understand the right side, you'll begin to see the differences more clearly. Most people don't even know there is a difference. They just assume that everything is risky, and they pay for it. But as the years go on and you become more comfortable with your experience and education on the right side, your vision will improve and you will begin to see what people on the left side cannot see. And you will understand why seeking security to avoid risk is the riskiest thing you can do. You'll develop your own financial vision and not have to accept other people's opinions. You'll be able to see for yourself and know the difference between financial facts and financial opinions."

It was a good day. In fact, it was one of the better lessons I could remember. It was great because it began to open my mind to things my eyes could not see.

Numbers Reduce Risk

Without those simple lessons from my rich dad, I doubt if I could have taken my passion and built the educational system of my dreams. Without his insistence on financial literacy and accuracy, I know I could not have invested as wisely, with so little of my own money, and earned such high returns. I always remember that, the bigger the project and the faster you want to succeed, the more you need to be accurate. If you want to get rich slowly, or just work all your life and let someone else manage your money, then you do not need to be as accurate. The faster you want to get rich, the more accurate with numbers you must be.

The good news is that, due to advances in technology and new products, it is much easier today to learn the necessary skills for building your own system and quickly developing your financial literacy.

You Can Go Fast, but Don't Take Shortcuts

- "To reduce your taxes, buy a bigger house and get deeper into debt so you can get a tax write-off."

- "Your home should be your largest investment."

- "You'd better buy now because the prices always go up."

- "Get rich slowly."

- "Live below your means."

If you take the time to study and learn about the subjects required for the right side of the CASHFLOW Quadrant, such statements won't make much sense. It might make sense to someone on the left side, but not to someone on the right. You can do anything you like, go as fast as you like, make as much money as you like, but you have to pay the price. You can go quickly, but remember, there are no shortcuts.

This book is not about answers. This book is about looking at financial challenges and objectives from a different point of view. It's not that one point of view is better than another. It's simply smarter to have more than one point of view.

In reading the following chapters, you may begin looking at finances, business, and life from a different point of view.

Chapter Eight
HOW DO I GET RICH?

If you do what everyone else does,
you'll wind up having what everyone else has.

When I'm asked, "Where did you learn your formula for getting rich?" I reply, "Playing *Monopoly* as a kid."

Some people think I'm kidding and wait for the punch line. But it is no joke. The formula for getting rich in *Monopoly* is simple, and it works in real life as well as in the game.

Four Green Houses… One Red Hotel

You may recall that the secret to wealth when playing *Monopoly* is simply to buy four green houses and then trade up for a large red hotel. That is all it takes. Kim and I took that same investment formula, applied it to real life, and grew wealthy and financially free.

When the real estate market was really bad, we bought as many small houses as we could with the limited money we had. When the market improved, we traded in the four green houses and bought a large red hotel. We never have to work again because the cash flow from our large red hotel, apartment houses, and mini-storages units pays for our lifestyle.

It Works for Hamburgers Also

Or if you don't like real estate, all you have to do is make hamburgers, build a business around that hamburger, and franchise it. Within a few years, the increasing cash flow will provide you with more money than you can spend.

In reality, that is how simple the path to extraordinary wealth is. In other words, in this high-tech world, the principles of great wealth remain simple and low-tech. I would say that it's merely common sense. But too often, when it comes to the subject of money, common sense is uncommon.

For example, it makes no sense to me to give people a tax break to lose money and spend their lives in debt. Or to call your home an asset when it really is a liability that drains cash from you every day. Or to have a national government that spends more money than it collects in taxes. Or to send a child to school to study so they can get a good job, but not to teach that child anything about money.

It Is Easy to Do What Rich People Do

Doing what rich people do is easy. One of the reasons there are so many wealthy people who didn't do well in school is because the "to-do" part of becoming wealthy is simple. You don't have to go to school to become rich. The "to-do" part of becoming rich is definitely not rocket science.

There is a classic book I recommend that you read: *Think and Grow Rich* by Napoleon Hill. I read this book as a youngster, and it greatly influenced the direction of my life.

There's a good reason why it's titled *Think and Grow Rich* and not "Work Hard and Grow Rich" or "Get a Job and Grow Rich." The fact is that people who work the hardest do not wind up rich. If you want to be rich, you need to think independently rather than go along with the crowd. In my opinion, one great asset of the rich is that they think differently than everyone else. If you do what everyone else does, you'll wind up having what everyone else has. And for most people, what they have is years of hard work, unfair taxes, and a lifetime of debt.

When someone asks me, "What do I have to do to move from the left side of the CASHFLOW Quadrant to the right side?" my response is, "It's not what you have to do that needs to change. It's first how you think that needs to change." In other words, it's who you have to be in order to do what needs to be done.

Do you want to be the kind of person who thinks buying four green houses and turning them in for one red hotel is easy? Or do you want to be the kind of person who thinks buying four green houses and turning them in for one red hotel is hard?

Years ago, I took a class on goal-setting. It was the mid-1970s, and I really could not believe I was spending

$150 and a beautiful Saturday and Sunday to learn how to set goals. I would rather have gone surfing. Instead, I was paying someone to teach me how to set goals. I nearly backed out several times, but what I learned from that class has helped me achieve what I want in life. The instructor put up on the board these three words:

BE
DO
HAVE

She explained, "Goals are the 'have' part of these three words: goals such as to have a nice body, or to have the perfect relationship, or to have millions of dollars. Once most people figure out their goal and what they want to have, they begin listing what they have to do in order to achieve the goal. That's why most people have to-do lists. They set their goal and then begin doing."

Using the goal of a perfect body, the instructor talked about the approach most people take: "What most people do when they want a perfect body is go on a diet and then go to the gym. This lasts for a few weeks and then most are back to their old diet of French fries and pizza. Instead of going to the gym, they watch baseball on TV. This is an example of doing instead of being.

"It's not the diet that counts. It's who you have to be to follow the diet that counts. Yet, every year millions of people seek the perfect diet in order to become thin. They focus on what they have to do, rather than who they have to be. A diet won't help if your thoughts do not change."

She used golf as another example: "Many people buy a new set of golf clubs hoping that they can improve their game, instead of first adopting the attitude, mindset, and beliefs of a good golfer. A lousy golfer with a new set of golf clubs is still a lousy golfer."

Then she discussed investments: "Many people think that buying stocks or mutual funds will make them rich. But simply buying stocks, mutual funds, real estate, and bonds won't make you rich. Just doing what professional investors do does not guarantee financial success. A person who has a loser mentality will always lose no matter what stock, bond, real estate, or mutual fund they buy."

A common goal people have is to find the perfect romantic partner, but according to the instructor, most people go about it all wrong. "So many people look everywhere for the perfect person, the person of their dreams. They look for the right person instead of working to become the right person."

And when they finally find this "perfect" person, they then try to change them. The instructor suggested that the answer lies within. To improve your marriage, you don't need to change your partner. It is better to change yourself first. "Don't work on the other person. Work on your thoughts about that other person."

As she talked about relationships, my mind drifted to the many people I've met over the years who were out to change the world, but weren't getting anywhere.

They wanted to change everyone else, but not change themselves.

I snapped out of my daydream when she started talking about money: "When it comes to money, many people try to do what the rich do and to have what the rich have. So they buy a house that looks rich, a car that looks rich, and send their kids to the schools where the rich send their kids. All this does is force these people to work even harder, which is not what the truly rich do."

I was nodding my head in agreement in the back of the room. My rich dad did not use those same words, but he often said, "People think that working hard for money and then buying things that make them look rich will make them rich. In most cases it doesn't. It only makes them more tired. They call it 'Keeping up with the Joneses.' And if you notice, the Joneses are exhausted."

During that weekend class, much of what my rich dad told me began to make more sense. For years he lived modestly, and instead of working hard to pay bills, he worked hard to acquire assets. If you saw him on the street, he looked like everyone else. He drove a pickup truck, not an expensive car. Then one day, when he was in his late thirties, he emerged as a financial powerhouse. People took notice when he suddenly bought one of the prime pieces of real estate in Hawaii. It was only after his name hit the paper that people realized that this quiet unpretentious man owned many other businesses and lots of prime real estate—and that when he spoke, his bankers listened. Few people ever saw the modest house he lived in. After he was flush with cash and cash flow from his assets, he bought a new large house for his family. He didn't take out a loan. He paid cash.

After that weekend class on goal-setting, I realized that many people tried doing what they thought the rich did, and tried having what the rich had. They would buy big houses and invest in the stock market because that's what they thought the rich did. Yet what my rich dad was trying to tell me was that, if they still had the thoughts, beliefs, and "ideas of a poor or middle-class person and did what the rich did, they would still wind up having what the poor and middle class have.

"Be-Do-Have" began to make sense.

The CASHFLOW Quadrant Is about Being, Not Doing

Moving from the left side of the CASHFLOW Quadrant to the right side is not so much about doing, but about being. It is not so much what the B or I does that makes the difference. It is how they think and who they are at their core being.

The good news is that it does not cost much money to change your thinking. In fact, it can be done for free. The bad news is that sometimes it's hard to change your deep core beliefs about money that are handed down from generation to generation, or learned from friends, work, and school. But it can be done. And that's what this book is primarily about.

It's not so much a how-to book on what to do to become financially free. And it's not about which stocks to buy or which mutual fund is safest. This book is about strengthening your thoughts (being) so that you can take the action (doing) that will enable you to become financially free (having).

Security Is the Issue for E's

Generally, people who seek out the E quadrant greatly value security. For them, it is often true that money is not as important as security. They may take great risks in other areas of their lives, but not when it comes to money.

Perfectionism Is the Issue for S's

This is a generalization, but what I have observed among people who are currently in the S quadrant but are trying to switch to the right side is the do-it-yourself mentality. They like to do it themselves because they have a great need to make sure things are done correctly. In their minds, the only way to ensure that things are done right is to do everything themselves.

For many S's, the real issue is their need to be in control. They hate making mistakes, but what they hate even more is someone else making mistakes and making them look bad. This makes them excellent S's and is why you hire them to do certain tasks. You want your dentist to be a perfectionist. You want your attorney to be a perfectionist. You want your brain surgeon to be a perfectionist. That is what you pay them for. That is their strength, but it's also their weakness.

Emotional Intelligence

A big part of being a human being is being human. And being human means having emotions. We all feel fear, sadness, anger, love, hate, disappointment, joy, happiness, and other emotions. What makes us individuals is how we handle those emotions.

When it comes to risking money, we all experience fear, even the rich. The difference is how we handle that fear. For many people, that emotion of fear generates the thought: "Play it safe. Don't take risks."

For others, especially those on the right side, the fear of losing money makes them think: "Play it smart. Learn to manage risk."

Same emotion, different thought: different being— different doing—different having.

The Fear of Losing Money

In my opinion, the greatest cause of human financial struggle is the fear of losing money. Because of this fear, people often operate too safely, or with too much personal control, or they just give their money to someone they think is an expert and hope and pray that the money will be there when they need it.

If fear keeps you prisoner in one of the financial quadrants, I recommend reading *Emotional Intelligence* by Daniel Goleman. In his book, Goleman explains the age-old puzzle of why people who do well in school do not always do well in the real world. His answer is that your emotional IQ is more powerful than your academic IQ. That is why people who take risks, make mistakes, and recover often do better than people who learned not to make mistakes and are afraid of risk. Too many people leave school with passing grades, yet are not emotionally prepared to take risks, especially financial ones. The reason so many teachers are not rich is because they operate in an environment that punishes people who make mistakes. Instead, to be financially free, we need to learn how to make mistakes and manage risk.

If people spend their lives terrified of losing money, afraid of doing things differently from what the crowd does, then getting rich is almost impossible, even if it is as simple as buying four green houses and trading them in for one large red hotel.

Emotional IQ Is Stronger

After reading Goleman's book, I came to realize that financial IQ is 90 percent emotional IQ and only 10 percent technical information about finance or money. Goleman quotes 16th-century humanist Erasmus of Rotterdam, who wrote in a satirical vein of the perennial tension between reason and emotion. In his writing, he uses the ratio of 24:1 in comparing the power of the emotional brain to the rational brain. In other words, when emotions are in high gear, they are 24 times stronger than the rational mind. Now I don't know if the ratio is scientifically valid, but it does have some usefulness to show the power of emotional thinking over rational thinking.

24 : 1
Emotional Brain : Rational Brain

All of us have experienced events in our lives when our emotions overtook our rational thoughts. I am certain most of us have:

- Said something out of anger that we later wished we had not said.

- Been attracted to someone we knew was not good for us, but still went out with them or, worse, married them.

- Have cried, or seen someone cry uncontrollably, because of the loss of a loved one.

- Done something intentionally to hurt someone we love because we were hurt.

- Had our heart broken and not gotten over it for a long time.

There are times when emotions are more than 24:1. This can be seen in:

- Addictions, such as compulsive eating, smoking, sex, shopping, drugs.

- Phobias, such as fear of snakes, heights, tight spaces, the dark, strangers.

These and other behaviors are often 100 percent emotionally driven. Rational thought has little power over the emotions when something as strong as addictions and phobias are involved.

Snakes Phobia

When I was in flight school, I had a friend with a snake phobia. During a class on how to survive in the wild after being shot down, the teacher brought out a harmless garden snake to show us how to eat it. My friend, a grown man, jumped up, screamed, and ran out of the room. He couldn't control himself. Not only was his phobia of snakes strong, but the idea of eating a snake was just too much for his emotions to bear.

Money Phobia

When it comes to risking money, I've seen people do the same thing. Instead of finding out about the investment, they also jump up, scream, and run out of the room.

Money manages to provoke many deep emotional phobias. I have them. You have them. We all have them.

Why? Because, like it or not, money is an emotional subject. And because it is an emotional subject, most people cannot think logically about money. If you don't think money is emotional, just watch the stock market. In most markets, there is no logic, only the emotions of greed and fear. Watch a person climb into a new car and smell the leather interior. All the salesperson has to do is whisper these magic words in their ear, "Low down payment. Easy monthly payments," and all logic goes out the window.

Emotional Thoughts Sound Logical

The problem with core emotional thoughts is that they sound logical. When someone in the E quadrant becomes fearful, their logical thought is: "Play it safe. Don't take risks." To someone in the I quadrant, however, that is not logical at all.

For people in the S quadrant, when the issue of trusting others to do a good job comes up, their logical thought may go like this: "I'll just do it myself."

That is why so many S-type businesses are often family businesses. There is a greater sense of trust. For them, blood is definitely thicker than water.

Different quadrants, different logic, different thoughts, different actions, different haves, same emotions.

What determines what we do is how we individually respond to emotions.

I Don't Feel Like It

One way to know if you're thinking emotionally instead of rationally is when you use the word "feel" in conversation. For example, many people who are run by their emotions say things like: "I don't feel like exercising today." Logically, they know they should exercise.

Many people who struggle financially are not able to control how they feel, or they let their feelings dictate their thoughts. I hear them say:

- "I don't feel like learning about investing. It's too much trouble."

- "Investing doesn't feel right for me."

- "I don't feel like telling my friends about my business."

- "I hate the feeling of being rejected."

Parent or Child

Those are thoughts generated from emotions, not logic. In pop psychology, it's the battle between the parent and child. The parent usually speaks in "should's." The parent says something like, "You should be doing your homework." The child speaks about "feeling" and responds to the parent by saying, "But I don't feel like doing it."

Financially, the parent in you would say silently, "You should save more money." But the child in you would reply, "But I really feel like taking a vacation. I'll just put the vacation on my credit card."

When Are You an Adult?

When going from the left side to the right side, we need to be adults. We all need to grow up financially. Instead of being parent or child, we need to look at money, work, and investing as adults. And what being an adult means is knowing what you have to do and doing it, even though you may not feel like doing it.

Conversations Within You

For people contemplating crossing from one quadrant to another, an important part of the process is to be aware and vigilant of your internal dialogue. Always remember that what sounds logical in one quadrant does not necessarily make sense in another. Going from financial security to financial freedom is primarily a process of changing your thinking. It's a process of doing your best to know which thoughts are emotion-based and which are logic-based. If you can keep your emotions in check and go for what you know to be logical, you have a good chance of making the journey. Ignore outside influences. The most important conversation is the one you are having with yourself.

When Kim and I were temporarily homeless and financially unstable, our emotions were out of control. Many times, what sounded logical was pure emotions talking. Our emotions were saying the same thing our friends were saying: "Play it safe. Get a secure job, and enjoy life."

But logically, we both agreed that freedom made more sense to us than security. In going for financial freedom, we knew we could find a sense of security that a job could never give us. The only things standing in our way were our emotionally driven thoughts. They sounded logical, but in the long term made no sense. The good news is that, once we made it across to the other side of the CASHFLOW Quadrant, the old thoughts stopped screaming and the new thoughts became our reality.

Today, I understand the emotions when a person says: "I can't take risks. I have a family to think about. I must have a secure job." Or "It takes money to make money. That's why I can't invest." Or "I'll do it on my own."

I feel their thoughts, for I have had those thoughts myself. But looking across the CASHFLOW Quadrant, having achieved financial freedom in the B and I quadrants, I can truly say that having financial freedom is a much more peaceful and secure way of thinking.

Differences between E and B

Core emotional values cause different points of view. The struggle in communication between business owners and employees is often caused by differences in emotional values. There has always been a struggle between the E and the B because one wants more pay, and the other wants more work. That is why we often hear: "I'm overworked and underpaid."

And from the other side we often hear: "What can we do to motivate them to work harder and be more loyal without paying them any more?"

Differences between B and I

There is also constant tension between business owners and the investors in that business, often called the shareholders. One wants more capital, and the other wants greater dividends.

A conversation at a shareholders meeting may sound like this:

Company managers: "We need a private jet so our executives can get to their meetings faster."

Investors: "We need fewer executives. Then we won't need a private jet."

Differences between S and B

In business transactions, I often see a bright S, such as an attorney, put a multimillion-dollar deal together for a B, a business owner. When the transaction is completed, the attorney becomes silently angry because the B makes millions and the S earns an hourly wage.

Their words may sound like this:

The attorney, the S, might say: "We did all the work, and he made all the money."

The business owner, the B, might say: "How many hours did those guys bill us for? We could have bought the whole law firm for what they charged."

Differences between E and I

Another example is a bank manager who gives an investor a loan to buy some real estate. The investor makes hundreds of thousands of tax-free dollars, and the banker gets a paycheck that is taxed heavily.

The bank manager, the E, might say: "I give that guy a loan, and he doesn't even say thank you. I don't think he knows how hard we worked for him."

The investor, the I, might say: "Boy, those guys are picky. Look at all this useless paperwork we have to do just to get a lousy loan."

Emotionally Volatile Marriage

The most emotionally volatile marriage I have ever witnessed was a couple where the wife was a hard-core E who believed in a job for financial security, while the husband fancied himself a high-flying I. He thought he was a future Warren Buffett but, in reality, he was an S—a commission-only salesman by profession, and a chronic gambler at heart. He was always looking for the investment that would help him get rich quick. He was all ears for any new stock offering, offshore investment scheme that promised ultra-high returns, or a real estate deal he could take an option on. This couple is still together, but I really don't know why. Each drives the other nuts. One person thrives on risk; the other hates risk. Different quadrants. Different core values.

If You Are Married or in a Primary Relationship

If you are married or in a primary relationship, circle the quadrant you generate the majority of your income from. Then circle the quadrant your spouse or partner generates income from.

The reason I ask you to do this is that the discussion between partners is often difficult if one partner doesn't understand where the other is coming from.

The Battle between the Rich and the Educated

There is another unspoken battlefield, and that is the difference in points of view between the educated and the rich.

In my years of researching the differences between the different quadrants, I often heard bankers, attorneys, accountants, and others like them grumble that they are the educated ones, and it is often the so-called less-educated person who makes the big bucks. This is the root of the battle between the educated and the rich. It's not that people in the B and I quadrants are uneducated, because many are highly educated. It's just that many B's and I's were not academic whiz kids in school.

For those of you who read my book *Rich Dad Poor Dad*, you know it's about the struggle between the educated and the rich. My highly educated but poor dad took great pride in the fact that he had years of advanced studies at prestigious schools like Stanford and the University of Chicago. My rich dad was a man who dropped out of school to run his family's business when his father died, so he never even finished high school. Yet he acquired tremendous wealth.

As I grew older and seemed to be more influenced by my rich but uneducated dad, my educated dad was occasionally defensive of his station in life. One day when I was about 16, my educated dad blurted out, "I have advanced degrees from prestigious schools. What does Mike's dad have?"

I paused and replied quietly, "Money, and free time."

More Than a Mental Change

As stated earlier, success in the B or I quadrant requires more than academic or technical knowledge. It often requires a change in core emotional thinking, feelings, beliefs, and attitude. Remember:

BE

DO

HAVE

What the rich do is relatively simple. It's the "be" that is different. The difference is found in their thoughts and, more specifically, their internal dialogue. That's why my rich dad forbade me from saying:

- I can't afford it.

- I can't do that.

- Play it safe.

- Don't lose money.

- What if you fail and never recover?

He banned those statements because he truly believed that words are powerful tools. What a person says and thinks becomes real.

Rich dad firmly believed that what we said to ourselves became our reality. That's why I suspect that, for people who struggle financially, their emotions often do the talking and control their lives. Until a person learns to overcome those emotionally driven thoughts, their words do become reality, words such as:

- I'll never be rich.

- That idea will never work.

- It's too expensive for me.

If they are emotionally based thoughts, they are powerful. The good news is that they can be changed with the support of new friends, new ideas, and a little time.

People who are not able to control their fear of losing should never invest on their own. They really are best served by turning that job over to a professional and not interfering with them.

I've met many professional people who are fearless when investing other people's money and able to make lots of money. But when it comes to investing or risking their own money, their fear of losing becomes too strong, and they ultimately lose. Their emotions do the thinking rather than their logic.

I've also met people who can invest their money and win constantly, but lose their calm when someone asks them to invest money for them.

The making and losing of money is an emotional subject, so my rich dad gave me the secret to handling these emotions. Rich dad always said, "To be successful as an investor or a business owner, you have to be emotionally neutral to winning and losing. Winning and losing are just part of the game."

Quitting My Secure Job

My friend Mike had a system that belonged to him. His father built it. I did not have that good fortune. I knew that someday I was going to have to leave the comfort and security of the nest and begin to build my own system.

In 1978 I resigned from my full-time secure job with Xerox and took the hard step forward with no safety net. The noise in my head from my fear and doubt was loud. I was nearly paralyzed with fear as I signed my letter of resignation, collected my last paycheck, and walked out the door. I had an orchestra of self-damaging thoughts and feelings playing inside me. I was bad-mouthing myself so loudly and with such conviction, that I couldn't hear anything else. It's a good thing, because so many of the people I worked with were saying: "He'll be back. He'll never make it."

The problem was that I was saying the same thing to myself. Those emotional thoughts of self-doubt haunted me for years—until Kim and I were successful in both the B and I quadrants. Today, I still hear those words. They just have less authority.

In the process of putting up with my own self-doubt, I learned to create other thoughts and statements of personal encouragement— statements such as: "Keep calm. Think clearly. Keep an open mind. Keep going. Ask someone who has gone before you for some guidance. Trust and keep the faith in a higher power wanting the best for you."

I learned to create these thoughts of encouragement internally, even though there was a part of me that was frightened and afraid.

I knew that I had little chance of success my first time out. But the positive emotions of trust, faith, and courage, along with good friends, moved me forward. I knew that I had to take risks. I knew that risk led to mistakes, and mistakes led to wisdom and knowledge, both of which I lacked. For me, failure would have been to let my fear win, so I was willing to move forward with few guarantees. My rich dad had instilled in me the idea that "failure is part of the process of success."

Internal Journey

The path from one quadrant to the next is an internal journey. It is a journey from one set of core beliefs and technical skills to a new set of core beliefs and skills. The process is much like learning to ride a bicycle. At first you fall down a lot. Often times it is frustrating and embarrassing, especially if your friends are watching. But after a while, the falling stops and riding becomes automatic. If you fall down again, it's not that big of a deal because you now know that you can get up and ride again. The process is the same when going from an emotional mindset of job security to the emotional mindset of financial freedom. Once Kim and I made the crossing, we were less afraid of failing because we were confident in our ability to stand back up again.

There are two statements that kept me going personally. One was my rich dad's words of advice when I was on the brink of quitting and turning back: "You can always quit. So why quit now?"

That statement kept my spirits higher and my emotions calm. It reminded me that I was halfway there, so why turn back? The distance going back was the same as going forward. It would be like Columbus quitting and turning back halfway across the Atlantic.

Sometimes quitting is the best move, and having the intelligence to know when to walk away is important. Too often I meet people who are so stubborn that they keep going forward on a project that has no chance of success. The problem of knowing when to quit or when to keep going is a common problem with anyone who takes risks. One way to manage this problem is to find mentors who have already successfully made the crossing before. A person who is already on the other side can best guide you. But be careful of advice from someone who has only read books about the crossing and gets paid to lecture on the subject.

The other statement that often kept me going was:

> "Giants often trip and fall,
> But worms don't, because
> All they do is dig and crawl."

The main reason so many people struggle financially isn't because they lack a good education or are not hardworking. It is because they are afraid of losing. If the fear of losing stops them, they've already lost.

Losers Cut Their Winners and Ride Their Losers

Fear of being a loser affects what people do in strange ways. I have seen people who bought stock at $20 sell their shares when they reached $30 because they were so afraid of losing what they had gained. And then they watched the stock go up to $100, split, and go up to $100 again.

Ironically, that same person who bought a stock at $20 will watch it go down to $3 and still hang on, hoping the price will come back up. This is an example of a person being so afraid of losing, or admitting they lost, that they wind up losing.

Winners Cut Their Losers and Ride Their Winners

Winners do things almost exactly the opposite. Often, the moment they know they took a losing position, i.e., their stock price starts to go down instead of up, they will sell and take their losses. Most are not ashamed to say they took a loss, because a winner knows that losing is part of the process of winning. When they find a winner, they will ride it up as far as it can go. The moment they know the free ride is over and the price has peaked, they cut and sell.

The key to being a great investor is to be neutral to winning and losing. Then you don't have emotionally driven thoughts, such as fear and greed, doing your thinking for you.

Losers Do the Same Things in Life

People who are afraid of losing do the same things in real life. We all know of:

- People who stay in marriages where there is no longer any love

- People who stay at dead-end jobs

- People who hang on to old clothes and things they never use

- People who stay in towns where they have no future

- People who stay friends with people who hold them back

Emotional Intelligence Can Be Controlled

Financial intelligence is closely linked to emotional intelligence. In my opinion, most people suffer financially because their emotions are in control of their thoughts. We as human BE-ings, all have the same emotions. What determines the differences between what we DO and what we HAVE in life is primarily how we handle those emotions.

For example, the emotion of fear can cause some of us to be cowards. But it also can spur others to become courageous. Unfortunately, when it comes to the subject of money, most people in our society are conditioned to be financial cowards. When the fear of losing money comes up, most people's minds automatically start chanting:

- "Security" rather than "Freedom"

- "Avoid risk" rather than "Learn to manage risk"

- "Play it safe" rather than "Play it smart"

- "I can't afford it" rather than "How can I afford it?"

- "It's too expensive" rather than "What is it worth long-term?"

- "Diversify" rather than "Focus"

- "What will my friends think?" rather than "What do I think?"

The Wisdom of Risk

There is a science to taking risks, especially financial risks. One of the best books I have read on the subject of money and risk management is *Trading for a Living* by Dr. Alexander Elder. Although it was written for people who professionally trade stocks and options, the wisdom of risk and risk management applies to all areas of money, money management, personal psychology, and investing.

One of the reasons many successful B's are not always as successful as I's is because they do not fully understand the psychology behind purely risking money. While B's understand risk when it involves business systems and people, that knowledge does not always translate into the systems of "money making money."

It's Emotional More Than Technical

In summary, moving from quadrants on the left to quadrants on the right is more emotional than technical. If people are not able to control their emotional thoughts, I don't recommend the journey.

The reason things look so risky on the right side to people on the left side is because the emotion of fear is often affecting their thinking. People on the left side think "play it safe" is a logical thought. It isn't. It's an emotional thought. And it's the emotional thoughts that keep people stuck in one quadrant or the other.

What people DO on the right side of the equation isn't that hard. I'm sincere when I say that it's as easy as buying four green houses for low prices, waiting until the market improves, selling them, and then buying a big red hotel.

Life really is a game of *Monopoly* for people on the right side of the CASHFLOW Quadrant. Sure, there is winning and losing, but that's just part of the game. Winning and losing are a part of life. To be successful on the right side is to BE a person who loves the game. Star athletes often lose more than they win, yet they love the game. Donald Trump went broke and battled back. He didn't quit because he lost. Losing only made him smarter and more determined. Many wealthy people went broke before they became rich. It's a part of the game.

If a person's emotions think for them, those emotional thoughts often blind them from seeing anything else. It's because of those knee-jerk emotional thoughts that people react, rather than think. And it's emotional thinking that causes people from different quadrants to argue. The arguments are caused by people not having the same emotional points of view. It's that emotional reaction that blinds a person from seeing how easy, and often risk-free, things are on the right side of the CASHFLOW Quadrant.

I encourage all of you who want to make the crossing to make sure you have a long-term positive support group and a mentor guiding you. The struggle Kim and I went through was worth it. For us, the most important thing about crossing from the left side to the right side was not what we had to do, but who we became in the process. To me, that is priceless.

Chapter Nine
BE THE BANK,
NOT THE BANKER

The rich create money.

I have focused on the BE portion of the formula BE—DO—HAVE because, without the proper mindset and attitude, you cannot be prepared for the great economic changes that are facing us today. By BEing someone with the skills and mindset of the right side of the CASHFLOW Quadrant, you will recognize opportunities that arise from these changes and be prepared to DO. This will lead you to HAVE financial success.

I remember a phone call I received from my rich dad in late 1986. "Are you in the real estate market or the stock market?" he asked. "Neither," I replied. "Everything I've invested is in building my business." "Good," he said. "Stay out of all markets. Keep building your business. Something big is about to happen."

That year, the U.S. Congress passed the Tax Reform Act of 1986. In just 43 days, Congress took away many of the tax loopholes that people counted on to shelter their income. For people who were using those "passive losses" from their income property as tax deductions, they suddenly still had their losses, but the government had taken away the tax deduction. All across America, real estate prices began to plunge, in some cases as much as 70 percent. Suddenly, property was worth far less than the amount of their mortgages. Panic swept the real estate market. Banks and savings and loans began to shake, and many failed. People could not get their money out of the banks, and then Wall Street crashed in October 1987. The world went into financial crisis.

Fundamentally, the Tax Reform Act of 1986 eliminated many of the tax loopholes that the high-income E's and S's depended upon. Many of them had invested in real estate properties or limited partnerships in order to utilize any losses to offset their earnings from the E or S quadrants. And while the crash and recession did affect people in the B and I quadrants, many of their tax-avoidance mechanisms were left intact.

During this period, E's learned a new word: downsizing. They soon realized that when a major layoff was announced, the share price of the stock of the company announcing the layoff went up. Sadly, most did not understand why. There were many S's also struggling to cope with the recession that was caused by decreased business, higher insurance rates, and losses from the real estate and stock markets. As a result, I believe that individuals on the left side of the CASHFLOW Quadrant were financially hurt and suffered the most as a direct result of the Tax Reform Act of 1986.

Transfer of Wealth

While people on the left side were suffering, many people on the B and I side were getting rich, thanks to the government taking away from some people and giving to others.

By changing the tax code, all the "tax-trick" reasons for investing were taken away from people who were simply buying real estate to lose money. Many were high-income employees or professionals such as doctors, attorneys, accountants, and small business owners. Prior to this period, they had so much taxable income that their advisors told them to buy real estate to lose money, and then with any extra money, invest in the stock market. When the government took that loophole away with the Tax Reform Act, one of the most massive transfers of wealth began. In my opinion, much of the wealth was taken away from the E and S side and handed to the B and I side for pennies on the dollar.

When the savings and loans (the organizations that issued the bad loans) failed, billions of dollars in deposits were at risk. The money had to be paid back. So who was left to pay back the billions of dollars lost in savings and real estate foreclosures? Well, the taxpayers of course, the very people who were already hurting enough as it was.

Some of you may remember a governmental agency called the Resolution Trust Corporation, or the RTC as it was commonly known. The RTC was the agency responsible for taking the foreclosures from the real estate crash and transferring them to people who knew how to handle them. For me and many of my friends, it was like a blessing from financial heaven.

Remember that money is seen with the mind, not with the eyes. During this period of time, emotions ran high and vision was blurred. People saw what they were trained to see. Three things happened to people on the left side of the CASHFLOW Quadrant:

1. Panic was everywhere. When emotions are high, financial intelligence often disappears. People were so concerned about their jobs, the falling value of their property, the crash of the stock market, and the general slowdown of business, that they failed to see the massive opportunities right in front of them. Their emotional thoughts blinded them. Instead of moving forward and beating the bushes, most people went into their caves and hid.

2. They lacked the technical skills required on the B and I side. Just as a doctor must have technical skills developed from years of schooling and then from on-the-job training, people in the B and I quadrants must also possess highly specialized technical skills. These include financial literacy, how to restructure debt, how to structure an offering, how to raise

capital, understanding your market, and other learnable skills.

When the RTC said, "We have a banker's box for sale, and in it is property that used to be worth $20 million, but you can have it today for $4 million," most E's and S's didn't have a clue about how to raise the $4 million to buy the gift from financial heaven or know how to recognize the good deals from the bad.

3. They lacked a cash machine. Most people during this period had to work harder just to survive. By operating as a B, my business could expand with little physical effort on my part. By 1990, my business was up and running and growing. During this period, the business grew from a start-up to 11 offices worldwide. The more it expanded, the less physical work I had to do, and the more money came in. The system and the people in the system were working hard. With the extra money and free time, Kim and I were able to spend a lot of time looking at deals. And there were many of them.

It Was the Best of Times... It Was the Worst of Times

There's a saying that goes: "It's not what happens in one's life that matters, but it's the meaning one puts on what happens that matters."

The period from 1986 to 1996 was, for some people, the worst time of their lives. For others, it was the best of times. When I received that phone call from my rich dad in 1986, I recognized the fantastic opportunity that this economic change presented me. Even though I did not have a lot of extra cash at the time, I was able to create assets by utilizing my skills as a B and an I. Later in this chapter, I will describe in greater detail how I created assets that helped me become financially free.

One of the keys to a successful and happy life is to be flexible enough to respond appropriately to whatever change comes your way. Unfortunately, most people are not equipped to handle the fast-breaking economic changes that have happened and continue to happen. However, most people are generally optimistic and have the ability to forget. After 10 to 12 years, they forget, and then things change again.

History Repeats Itself

Today, people have more or less forgotten about the Tax Reform Act of 1986. The E's and S's are working harder than ever. Why? Because their tax loopholes have been taken away.

As they have worked harder to get back what they lost, their incomes have gone up and their tax accountant has again started whispering the same old words of wisdom: "Go buy a bigger house. Interest on your debt is your best tax deduction. And besides, your home is an asset, and it should be your largest investment." So they look at "the easy monthly payments," and they get sucked into a higher debt position.

In my opinion, a great transfer of wealth is happening, and it may be happening in a very different way than we might expect. This is why my rich dad had me read books on economic history. Economies change, but history repeats.

And money continues to flow from the left side to the right side of the CASHFLOW Quadrant, just as it always has. Many people are deeply in debt, yet they pour money into the stock market, often through their retirement plans. The B's and I's on the right side will sell at the top of the market, just when the last cautious people on the left side overcome their fear and enter the market. Something newsworthy will happen, the market will crash, and when the dust settles, the investors will move back in. They will buy back what they just sold. Again, we will have another great transfer of wealth from the left side to the right side of the CASHFLOW Quadrant.

It will take many years to heal the emotional scars of those who lost money—but the wounds will heal, just as another market is nearing its peak.

At about that time, people will begin quoting Yogi Berra, the great New York Yankees baseball player: "It's déjà vu all over again."

Is It a Conspiracy?

Often I hear people, especially E's and S's, say that there is some kind of global conspiracy held together by a few ultra-rich families who control the banks. These conspiracy theories have been around for years.

Is there a conspiracy? I don't know. Could there be a conspiracy? Anything is possible. I know there are powerful families who control massive sums of money. But does one group control the world? I see it as one group of people on one side with one mindset, and another group of people on the other side with a different mindset. They are all playing this one big game of money, but each quadrant is playing from a different point of view and with a different set of rules.

The big problem is that the people on the left side are unable to see what the people on the right side are doing. But the people on the right side know exactly what the people on the left side are doing.

Witch Hunts

Instead of finding out what the people on the right side know, E's and S's often go on witch hunts. Only a few centuries ago when there was a plague or something bad happened to a community, townspeople would go on a witch hunt. They needed someone to blame for their plight.

Well, witch hunts still go on today. Many people look for someone to blame for their financial problems. These people often want to blame the rich for their problems rather than admit that their own lack of information about money often is a fundamental reason for their struggles.

Heroes Become Villains

Every few years, a new financial guru appears and seems to have some new magic formula for wealth. In the late 1970s, it was the Hunt brothers who tried to corner the silver market. The world initially applauded their genius, but almost overnight they were hunted down as criminals because so many people lost money after they followed the brothers' advice. In the late 1980s, it was Michael Milken, the junk-bond king. One day he was a financial genius, but right after the crash, he was tracked down and sent to jail. Individuals change, but history repeats.

Today we have new investment geniuses. They are all over TV, the Internet, and financial publications. Some have even attained celebrity status. Warren Buffett is touted as a near god. When he buys something, everybody rushes in and buys what he buys. And when Warren Buffett sells, prices crash. Money follows him freely. If there is a major market correction in the near future, will today's financial heroes be tomorrow's hated villains? Time will tell.

In every up cycle of the economy, there are heroes. And in every down period, there are villains. Often they end up being the same people. People will always need witches to burn or conspiracies to blame for their own financial blindness. History will repeat itself, and again a great transfer of wealth will take place. When it does, which side of the transfer will you be on: the left side, or the right side?

In my opinion, people simply fail to realize that they are in this large global game, a virtual casino in the sky, but no one ever told them that they are important players in the game. The game is called "Who Is Indebted to Whom?"

Be the Bank, Not the Banker

When I was in my mid-twenties, it dawned on me that the name of the game was to be the bank, but that didn't mean to get a job as a banker. My advanced education was about to begin. It was during this period that my rich dad had me look up words like "mortgage," "real estate," and "finance." I was beginning to train my mind to see what my eyes could not.

He encouraged me to understand the game and, when I learned the game, I could do what I wanted with what I found. I decided to share my knowledge with anyone who was interested.

He also had me read books on the great leaders of capitalism—people such as John D. Rockefeller, J. P. Morgan, and Henry Ford. One of the most important books I read was *The Worldly Philosophers* by Robert Heilbroner. For people who want to operate on the B and I side, his book is a must-read, for it traces the greatest economists of all time, starting with Adam Smith who wrote *The Wealth of Nations*. It is fascinating to look into the minds of some of our most important philosophers, the economists. These people interpreted the evolution of modern capitalism over its brief history. In my opinion, if you want to be a leader on the B and I side, a historical view of economic history is important to understanding both our history and our future.

After *The Worldly Philosophers,* I recommend reading *The Creature from Jekyll Island* by G. Edward Griffin, Paul Zane Pilzer's *Unlimited Wealth,* James Dale Davidson's *The Sovereign Individual,* Robert Preacher's *The Crest of the Wave,* and Harry Dent's *The Great Depression Ahead.* While Heilbroner's book gives you insight into where we have come from economically, the other authors give their views on where we are headed. Their contrasting viewpoints have been important. They allowed me to see what my eyes could not. By reading books like these, I have been able to gain insights into the ups and downs, the cycles and trends, of the economy. A common theme in all of these books is that one of the biggest changes of all is right around the corner.

How to Play the Bank

After the 1986 Tax Reform Act became law, there were opportunities everywhere. Real estate, stocks, and businesses were available for low prices. While it was devastating for many people on the left side, it was wonderful for me because I could utilize my skills as a B and I to take advantage of the opportunities around me. Instead of being greedy and chasing everything that looked like a good deal, I decided to focus on real estate.

Why real estate? For these five simple reasons:

1. **Pricing**

   Real estate prices were so low that mortgage payments were far lower than the fair-market rent for most properties. These properties made great economic sense, which meant there was little risk. It was like going to a sale at a retail store when everything was 50 percent off.

2. **Financing**

   The banks would give me a loan on real estate, but not on stocks. Since I wanted to buy as much as I could while the market was depressed, I bought real estate so that what cash I had could be combined with financing through banks.

   For example, let's say I had $10,000 in savings to invest. If I bought stocks, I could only buy $10,000 worth of stocks. I could have bought on margin and put up only part of the total cost and the broker company would have loaned me the remainder, but I wasn't financially strong enough to risk a downturn in the market.

   With $10,000 in real estate and a 90 percent loan, I could buy a $100,000 property.

   If both markets went up 10 percent, I would have made $1,000 in stocks, but $10,000 in real estate.

3. **Taxes**

   If I made $1 million in profit from stocks, I'd have to pay nearly 30 percent in capital-gains tax on my profit. But in real estate, the $1 million profit could be rolled tax-free into the next real estate transaction. On top of that, I could depreciate the property for even greater tax advantages.

   Important note: An investment must make economic sense outside of the tax benefit for me to invest in it. Any tax benefit only makes the investment more attractive.

4. **Cash flow**

   Rents had not declined, even though real estate prices had declined. This put a lot of money in my pocket, paid for the mortgages and, most importantly, bought me time to wait until real estate prices went up again. When they did, I was able to sell. Although I carried large debt, it never hurt me because the rents were far greater than the cost of carrying the loan.

5. **An opportunity to become a bank**

   Real estate allowed me to become a bank, something I had wanted to do since 1974.

The Rich Create Money

In *Rich Dad Poor Dad,* I wrote about how the rich create money and often play the role of banker. The following is a simple example that almost anyone can follow.

Let's say I find a house worth $100,000 and I get a heck of a deal and only pay $80,000 for it. I pay a $10,000 down payment and get a $70,000 mortgage I'm responsible for.

I then advertise that the house is available for sale for its appraised price of $100,000. I use these magic words in the ad: "House for sale. Owner desperate. No bank qualifying. Low down payment. Easy monthly payments."

The phone rings like crazy. The house is sold on what is called a "wrap" or a lease-purchase contract. In simple terms, I sell the house for a $100,000 IOU. This is what the transaction looks like:

MY BALANCE SHEET

Assets	Liabilities
$100,000 IOU	**$70,000 Mortgage**

BUYER'S BALANCE SHEET

Assets	Liabilities
	$100,000 IOU

This transaction is then registered with a title and escrow office, which often handles the payments. If the person defaults on the $100,000, I simply foreclose and sell the property to the next person who wants a "low down payment, easy monthly payment" home to live in. People line up for the opportunity to buy a home on these terms.

The net effect is that I have created $30,000 in my asset column for which I am paid interest, just like a bank gets paid interest for the loans it makes.

I was beginning to be a bank, and I loved it. Remember that rich dad said, "Be careful when you take on debt. If you take on debt personally, make sure it's small. If you take on large debt, make sure someone else is paying for it."

In the language of the B and I side, I "laid off" my risk, or "hedged" my risk to another buyer. That is the game in the world of finance.

This type of transaction is done all over the world. Yet wherever I go, people come up to me and say those magic words: "You can't do that here."

What most small investors fail to realize is that many large commercial buildings are bought and sold exactly in the manner described above. Sometimes they go through a bank, but many times they do not.

It's Like Saving $30,000 without Saving

I previously wrote about why the government does not give people a tax advantage for saving money. Well, I doubt if the banks will ever ask the government to do so because your savings are their liability.

The United States has a low savings rate simply because banks do not want your money or need your savings to do well. So this example is a way of playing bank and increasing your savings without a great deal of effort.

The cash flow from this $30,000 is reflected as follows:

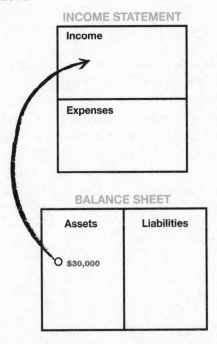

There are several interesting things about this diagram:

1. I determine the interest rate for my $30,000. Often it's 10 percent interest. Most banks pay you less than 5 percent on your savings today. So even if I did use my own $10,000 as a down payment, which I try not to do, the interest on it is often better than the bank would pay me.

2. It's like creating $20,000 ($30,000 less the $10,000 down payment) that didn't exist before, just like the bank creates an asset and then charges interest on it.

3. This $20,000 was created tax-free. For the average person in the E quadrant, it would take nearly $40,000 of wages to be able to set aside $20,000. Income earned as an employee is a 50–50 proposition, with the government taking its 50 percent through withholding tax before you ever see it.

4. All property taxes, maintenance, and management fees are now the responsibility of the buyer because I sold the property.

And there is more. Many creative things can be done on the B and I side to create money from nothing, just by playing the role of the bank.

A transaction like this may take a week to a month to put together. The question is: How long would it take for most people to earn an additional $40,000 so they can save $20,000 after taxes and other expenses?

The Income Stream Is Sheltered

In *Rich Dad Poor Dad*, I briefly covered why the rich use corporations:

1. **Asset protection**

    If you are rich, people tend to want to take what you have through litigation. But the rich often don't own anything in their own names. Their assets are held in trusts and corporations to protect them.

2. **Income protection**

    By passing the income stream from assets through your own corporation, much of the income that is normally taken from you by the government through taxes can be sheltered.

The harsh reality is that, for employees, the sequence goes like this:

As an employee, your earnings are taxed and taken through withholding taxes even before you get your paycheck. So if an employee is paid $30,000 per year, by the time the government gets through with it, it's down to $15,000. With this $15,000, you must then pay your mortgage and all your other daily expenses.

If you pass your income stream through a corporate entity first, this is what the pattern would look like:

EARN

↓

SPEND

↓

TAXED

By passing the income stream from the $30,000 through a corporation, you can expense much of the earnings before the government gets their hands on it. If you own the corporation, you make the rules, as long as it conforms to the tax code.

For example, if you make the rules, you can write into the bylaws of your company that child care is part of your employment package. The company may pay $400 per month for child care out of pre-tax dollars. If you pay for it with after-tax dollars, you have to effectively earn almost $800 to pay for that same child care. The list is long and the requirements are specific as to what an owner of a corporation can write off that an employee cannot. Certain travel expenses can be written off with pre-tax dollars as long as you can document that you conducted business, such as a board meeting, on the trip. Just make sure you follow the rules. Even retirement plans are different for owners and employees, in many instances. Having said all of this, I want to stress that you must follow the required regulations to make these expenses deductible. I believe in taking advantage of the legal deductions allowed by the tax code, but I do not recommend breaking the law.

Again, the key to taking advantage of some of these provisions is which quadrant you earn your income from. If all of your income is generated as an employee from a company that you don't own or control, there's little income or asset protection available to you.

That is why I recommend that, if you're an employee, keep your job, but begin to spend time in the B or I quadrants. Your road to faster freedom is through those two quadrants. To feel more financially secure, the secret is to operate in more than one quadrant.

Free Land

A while back, Kim and I wanted some property away from the hustle and bustle of the crowded city. We got the urge to own some acreage with tall oak trees and a stream running through it. We also wanted privacy.

We found a 20-acre parcel priced at $75,000. The seller was willing to take 10 percent down and carry the balance at 10 percent interest. It was a fair transaction. The problem was that it violated the rule on debt that rich dad taught me, which was: "Be careful when you take on debt. If you take on debt personally, make sure it's small. If you take on large debt, make sure someone else pays for it."

We passed on the $75,000 piece of land and went looking for property that made more sense. To me, $75,000 is a lot of debt because our cash flow would have looked like the next diagram:

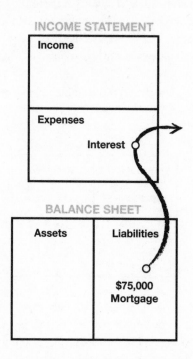

And remember rich dad's rule: "If you take on debt and risk, then you should be paid." Well, in this transaction, I would have taken on both the debt and the risk, and I was the one paying for it.

About a month later, we found a piece of land for $115,000 that was even more beautiful. It was 87 acres of tall oak trees with a stream, and it had a house. I offered the seller full price if he would give me my terms, which he did. To make a long story short, we spent a few dollars fixing the house and sold the house and 30 acres for $215,000, using the same idea of "low down payment, easy monthly payments." We kept 57 acres for ourselves.

This is what the transaction looked like on my balance sheet:

BALANCE SHEET

Assets	Liabilities
$215,000	$115,000

The new owner was thrilled because it was a beautiful home and he was able to buy it for almost nothing down. As an aside, he also bought it through his company for use as a corporate retreat for his employees, which allowed him to depreciate the purchase price as a company asset, deduct the maintenance costs, and deduct the interest payments. His interest payments more than paid for my interest payments. A few years later, he sold some of his company stock and paid off the loan to me, and I, in turn, paid off my loan. The debt was gone.

With the extra $100,000 profit I made, I was able to pay the taxes from the gain of the land and the house.

The net result was zero debt, $15,000 profit after taxes, and 57 acres of gorgeous land. It was like being paid for getting what you want.

Today, my balance sheet from that one transaction looks like this:

BALANCE SHEET

Assets	Liabilities
57 acres land $15,000 cash	

The IPO

An initial public offering (IPO), or taking a private company public through a stock offering, is based on the same principles as the transaction described in the previous section. While the words, the market and, the players are different, the basic underlying principles remain the same. When my organization forms a company to take public, we often create value out of thin air, even though we try to base it on an accurate opinion of the fair market value. We take the offering to the public market and, instead of this equity being sold to one person, it is sold to thousands of people as shares of a company.

The Value of Experience

I recommend people start in the B quadrant before proceeding to the I quadrant. Regardless of whether the investment is in real estate, a business, stocks, or bonds, there is an underlying comprehensive business sense that is essential to being a sound investor. Some people have this comprehensive sense, but many do not, primarily because school trains us to be highly specialized, not comprehensively trained.

For those thinking about moving to the B or I quadrants, I recommend starting small and taking your time. Do bigger deals as your confidence and experience grow. Remember, the only difference between an $80,000 deal and an $800,000 deal is a zero. The process of going through a small deal is much the same as going through a much larger, multimillion-dollar public offering. It is only a matter of more people, more zeros, and more fun.

Once a person gains experience and a good reputation, it takes less and less money to create bigger and bigger investments. Many times it takes no money to make a lot of money. Why? Experience is valuable. As stated earlier, if you know how to make money with money, people and money will flock to you. Start small, and take your time. Experience is more important than money.

It Is Simple and Easy

In theory, the numbers and transactions on the right side of the CASHFLOW Quadrant are simple, regardless of whether we're talking about stocks, bonds, real estate, or businesses. To be financially well off simply means being able to think differently, to think from different quadrants and to have the courage to do things differently. To me, one of the hardest things a person who is new to this way of thinking has to go through is the countless number of people who will tell you: "You can't do that."

If you can overcome that kind of limited thinking and seek out people who say to you, "Yes, I know how to do that. I'd be happy to teach you," your life will be much easier.

The Laws

I started this chapter with the Tax Reform Act of 1986. While that was a significant rule change, it won't be the last. I only use the Tax Reform Act as an example of how powerful some rules and laws can be. If a person is to be successful in the B or I quadrant, he or she needs to be aware of market forces and any changes in the law that affect those market forces.

Today in America there are thousands upon thousands of pages of tax law. That's just for the IRS alone. The federal laws come to more than 1.2 million pages of laws. It would take the average reader 23,000 years to read the entire U.S. IRS Code. Every year more laws are created, repealed, or amended. It would be more than a full-time job just to keep up with the amendments.

Every time someone tells me, "That's against the law," I reply by asking them if they have read every line of code in America. If they say yes, I leave slowly, backing up toward the door. Never turn your back on someone who thinks they know every law.

To be successful on the right side requires seeing five percent with your eyes and 95 percent with your mind. Understanding the laws and market forces is vital for financial success. Great transfers of wealth often occur when laws and markets change, so it is important to pay attention if you want to have those changes work in your favor, and not against you.

The Government Needs Your Money

I believe in paying taxes. I know the government provides many important and vital services essential for a well-run civilization. Unfortunately, in my opinion, government is too big, mismanaged, and has made too many promises it cannot keep. But it's not only the fault of the politicians and lawmakers in office today. Most of the financial problems we face today were created by their predecessors. Unfortunately, if lawmakers want to keep their jobs, they can't tell the public the truth. If they did, they'd be thrown out of office because the masses still depend on the government to solve their financial and medical problems. Government cannot.

In the meantime, government will have to continue to increase taxes, even if the politicians promise not to. That's why Congress passed the Tax Reform Act of 1986. It needed to plug a tax loophole in order to collect more in taxes. Many Western governments must continue to collect even more taxes to prevent a default on some of those promises made long ago, such as Medicare and Social Security, as well as federal pensions for millions of federal workers.

As the deficit grows, retirement funds (401(k) plans in America or superannuation funds in many other countries) will begin to shrink because they are subject to market fluctuations. Mutual funds will begin to liquidate their stocks in order to pay for the sell orders from baby boomers who need to use the money for retirement. Baby boomers will suddenly be stuck with huge capital-gains taxes from the gains accrued by these mutual funds and taxable to them on withdrawal. The capital gains will come from selling these overvalued stocks at higher prices, which the funds pass on to its members. Instead of cash, many baby boomers will be stuck with a tax bill for capital gains they never received. Remember, the tax man always gets the money first.

Simultaneously, the health of millions of poorer baby boomers will begin to fail because poor people historically have worse health than affluent people. Medicare will be bankrupt, and the cry for more government support will go up in cities all across America.

Add to this the eclipsing of America by China as the nation with the largest GDP and the trend toward pushing services (such as accounting, information technology, and telesales) to nations such as India, and it becomes clear that wages will have to come down or productivity must skyrocket in order to meet the challenges of our rapidly changing global marketplace.

The next great transfer of wealth is taking place by ignorance. The Industrial Age's entitlement mentality of big government and big business should be on its way out. But here we are, in the midst of the Information Age, and we are grasping at old solutions to new world problems.

In 1989, the Berlin Wall came down. As stated earlier, in my opinion, that event was as significant as the year 1492 when Columbus bumped into the Americas in his search for Asia. In some circles, 1492 was the official beginning of the almost 500-year Industrial Age. The end was marked in 1989. The rules have changed.

History Is a Guide

My rich dad encouraged me to learn the game well. After I learned it well, I could do what I wanted with what I knew. I write and teach out of concern that more people need to know how to take care of themselves financially and not become dependent upon the government or a company for life support.

I hope I'm wrong about what I see coming down the road economically. Maybe governments can keep making promises to take care of people, keep on raising taxes, and keep on going into greater debt. Maybe the stock market will always go up and never come down again. And maybe real estate prices will go up again, and your home will become your best investment. And maybe millions of people will find happiness earning a minimum wage and be able to provide a good life for their family. Maybe this can all happen. But I don't think so. Not if history is any guide.

Historically, if people live to be 75 years of age, they live through two recessions and one depression. As baby boomers, we have gone through three recessions, and some question whether we are entering another depression. Maybe there will never be one, but history says there will. As the saying goes: "If your neighbor loses his job, it's a recession. If you lose your job, it's a depression."

The reason my rich dad had me read books on the great capitalists and the economists was so I could gain a longer view and a better perspective on where we have come from and where we are going.

Just as there are waves on the ocean, there are great waves in markets. Instead of the wind and sun driving the waves of the ocean, the waves of the financial markets are driven by two human emotions: greed and fear. I don't think that depressions are things of the past because we will always have those emotions of greed and fear. And when greed and fear collide and a person loses badly, the next human emotion is depression. Depression is made up of anger and sadness: anger with one's self, and sadness over the loss. Economic depressions are emotional depressions. People lose, and they get depressed.

Even when the economy appears to be in great shape, there are millions of people who are in various stages of depression. They may have a job, but deep down they know they are not getting ahead financially. They are angry at themselves and sad over their loss of time. Little do they know that they have been trapped by the Industrial-Age idea of "find a safe, secure job, and don't worry about the future."

A Great Change Means Opportunity

We are entering an era of tremendous change and opportunity. For some people, it will be the best of times. For others, it will be the worst of times.

As President John Kennedy once said: "A great change is at hand." Kennedy came from the right side of the CASHFLOW Quadrant. Back in the 1960s, he tried desperately to elevate the lives of those stuck in a time warp. Unfortunately, decades later, millions of people are still trapped in those time warps, following ideas that were handed down from past generations— ideas such as, "Go to school so you can find a secure job." While education is more important than ever before, we need to be teaching people to think a little further than just looking for a secure job and expecting the company or the government to look after them once their working days are through. That is an Industrial-Age idea, and we are not there anymore.

Nobody said it was fair, for this is not a fair country. We are a free country. There are people who work harder, are smarter, are more driven for success, are more talented, or are more desirous of the good life than others. In America, we are, thankfully, free to pursue those ambitions if we have the determination. Yet, every time somebody does better than we do, some people say it's unfair—the same people who think it would be more fair if the rich shared with the poor. Well, nobody said it was fair. And the more we try to make things fair, the less free we become.

When someone says to me that there is discrimination or a "glass ceiling," I agree with them. I know such things exist. I personally detest any kind of discrimination and, being of Japanese ancestry, I've experienced it firsthand. In the E and S quadrants, discrimination does exist, especially in companies. Your looks, your education, your skin color, and your gender all count on the left side. But they don't count on the right side, where fairness and security don't matter. It's all about freedom and the love of the game. If you want to play the game on the right side, the players will welcome you. If you play and win, fine. They will embrace you even more and ask you for your secrets. If you play and lose, they'll gladly take all your money. But don't complain or blame someone else for your failures. That is not the way the game is played on the right side. It's not meant to be fair. Being fair is not the name of the game.

Why Does Government Leave the B and I Quadrants Alone?

In reality, governments don't leave the B and I quadrants alone. It's more that the B and I quadrants have more ways of escaping and hiding wealth. In *Rich Dad Poor Dad,* I talked about the power of corporations. One big reason the rich keep more of their wealth is simply because they operate as corporate bodies, not human bodies. A human body needs a passport to go from country to country. A corporate body doesn't. A corporate body travels the world freely, and can often work freely. A human body needs to register with the government, and in America they need a "green card" to work. A corporate body doesn't.

While governments would like to take more money from corporate bodies, they realize that if they pass abusive tax laws, the corporate bodies will take both their money and their jobs to some other country. In the Industrial Age, people talked about offshore as a country. The rich have always sought tax havens where their money would be treated kindly.

Today, offshore is not a country. It's cyberspace. Money, being an idea and invisible, can now hide in the invisible electronic realm. Soon, if it is not already being done, people will do their banking on a geo-synchronous satellite orbiting in space free from any laws, or they may choose to operate in a country whose laws are more favorable to rich people.

In *Rich Dad Poor Dad*, I wrote that corporations became popular at the start of the Industrial Age just after Columbus discovered a new world filled with riches. Each time the rich sent a vessel out to sea, they were at risk because, if the ship didn't come back, the rich didn't want to be indebted to the families of sailors who died. So corporations were formed for legal protection and to limit the risk of loss to the amount of money ventured.

Wherever I travel in the world, the people I deal with primarily are employees of their own corporations. In theory, they own nothing and really don't exist as private citizens. They exist as officers of their rich corporations, but as private citizens they own nothing. And wherever I go in the world, I meet people who tell me, "You can't do that in this country. It's against the law."

Little do most people realize that most countries' laws in the Western world are similar. They may use different words, but in principle their laws are pretty much the same.

If possible, I recommend that you at least consider being an employee of your own corporation. It is especially advisable for high-income S's and B's, even if they own franchises or earn their income from network marketing. Seek advice from competent financial advisors to help you choose and implement the best structure for your particular situation.

There Are Two Kinds of Laws

On the surface, it seems as if there are laws for the rich and laws for everyone else. But in reality, the laws are the same. The only difference is that the rich use the laws to their advantage, while the poor and middle classes do not. That is the fundamental difference.

I strongly suggest hiring smart advisors, obeying the law, and making lots of money legally. Your legal advisors will serve as your early warning system for upcoming changes in the law. And when laws change, wealth changes hands.

Two Choices

One advantage of living in a free society is the freedom to make choices. In my opinion, there are two big choices: the choice of security, and the choice of freedom. If you choose security, you will pay a huge price for that security in the form of excessive taxes and punishing interest payments. If you choose freedom, then you need to learn the whole game and play it wisely. It's your choice which quadrant you want to play the game from.

Part I of this book defined the specifics of the CASHFLOW Quadrant, while Part II focused on developing the mindset and attitude of someone who chooses the right side of the B and I quadrants. By now, you should know which quadrant you are currently in and have an idea where you want to be. You also should have a better understanding of the mental process and mindset of operating from the right side of the CASHFLOW Quadrant.

While I have shown you ways to cross from the left side to the right side, it is now time to get specific. In the final section, I will identify seven steps to find the financial Fast Track that I consider essential in moving to the B and I quadrants.

Build Businesses, and Buy Real Estate

In 1943, the United States began taxing all working Americans via payroll deductions. In other words, the government got paid before people in the E quadrant got paid. Anyone who was purely an E had little escape from the government. It also meant that, instead of only the rich being taxed, which was the hope of the 16th Amendment, every E and S got taxed, rich or poor. Today the lowest wage-earners in America pay more in taxes, as a percentage of total income, than the rich and middle class.

In 1986, the Tax Reform Act went after the highly paid professionals in the S quadrant. This act specifically targeted doctors, lawyers, architects, dentists, engineers, and other professionals, and made it difficult, if not impossible, for them to shelter their income the way that the rich can do in the B and I quadrants.

These professionals were forced to operate their businesses through S corporations instead of C corporations, or else pay a tax penalty. The rich do not pay this penalty. Income for these highly compensated professionals is then passed through the S corporation and taxed at the highest individual tax rate possible. They do not have the opportunity to shelter their income through deductions allowed to C corporations. At the same time, the law was changed to force all S corporations to have a calendar year-end. This again forced all income to be taxed at the highest rate.

When I discussed these changes with my CPA, he reminded me that the biggest shock to newly self-employed people generally comes at the end of their first business year when they realize that the biggest tax they are paying is a self-employment tax. This tax is double for S's or self-employed, over what they paid as E's or employees. And it is calculated based on income before the individual can deduct any itemized deductions or personal exemptions. It is possible for a self-employed person to have no taxable income, yet still owe self-employment tax. Corporations, on the other hand, do not pay self-employment tax.

The 1986 Tax Reform Act also effectively pushed the E's and S's of America out of real estate as an investment and into paper assets such as stocks and mutual funds. Once the downsizing began, millions not only felt less secure about their jobs, they also felt less secure about their retirement, simply because their future financial well-being was based upon paper assets subject to the ups and downs of the market.

The 1986 Tax Reform Act also appears to have had the intention of shutting down the smaller community banks in America and shifting all banking to large national banks. I suspect that this was done so America could compete with the large banks of Germany and Japan. If that was the intent, it was successful. Today in America, banking is less personal and purely by the numbers. The net result is that it is harder for certain classes of people to qualify for home loans. Instead of a small-town banker knowing you personally, a central computer spits your name out if you don't meet its impersonal qualification requirements.

After the 1986 Tax Reform Act, the rich continue to earn more, work less, pay less in taxes, and enjoy greater asset protection by using the formula my rich dad gave me years earlier, which was, "Build a business, and buy real estate." The idea was to make a lot of money via C corporations, and shelter the income through real estate. While millions upon millions of Americans work, pay more and more in taxes, and then pour billions each month into mutual funds, the rich are quietly selling shares of their C corporations, making them even richer, and then buying billions in investment real estate. A share of a C corporation allows the buyer to share in the risk of owning the company. A share of stock does not allow the shareholder the advantages that owning a C corporation and investing in real estate offer.

Why did my rich dad recommend building businesses in C corporations and then buying real estate? Because the tax laws reward people who operate that way, but this subject is beyond the scope of this book. Just remember the words of immensely wealthy people such as Ray Kroc, founder of McDonald's: "My business is not hamburgers. My business is real estate." Or remember the words of my rich dad who drummed into my head, "Build businesses, and buy real estate."

In other words, I needed to seek my fortune on the right side of the CASHFLOW Quadrant to take full advantage of the tax laws.

In 1990, President George H. W. Bush raised taxes after promising, "Read my lips. No new taxes." In 1992, President Bill Clinton signed into law one of the largest tax increases in recent history. Tax increases continue into the 21st century. Again, these tax increases affect the E's and S's, but the B's and I's are, for the most part, not affected.

As we progress further and further into the Information Age, we all need to continue to gather information from different quadrants. In the Information Age, quality information is our most important asset. As Eric Hoffer once said: "In times of change, learners inherit the earth, while the learned

find themselves beautifully equipped to deal with a
world that no longer exists."

Remember

Everyone's financial situation is different. That is
why I always recommend the following:

1. Seek out the best professional and financial
    advice you can find. For example, while a
    C corporation works well in many instances,
    it is not the best structure all of the time.
    Even on the right side of the CASHFLOW
    Quadrant, occasionally an S corporation
    is appropriate.

2. Remember that there are different advisors
    for the rich, the poor, and the middle class,
    just as there are different advisors for people
    who earn their money on the right side and
    on the left. Also, consider seeking advice
    from people who are already where you want
    to go.

3. Never do business or investing for tax
    reasons. A tax break is an extra bonus for
    doing things the way the government wants.
    It should be a bonus, not the reason.

If you are not a U.S. citizen, this advice remains
the same. Our laws may be different, yet the
principles of seeking competent advice remain the
same. People on the right side operate very similarly
throughout the world.

Part Three

HOW TO BECOME A SUCCESSFUL B AND I

Chapter Ten
TAKE BABY STEPS

You've got to walk before you can run.

Most of us have heard the saying: "A journey of a thousand miles begins with a single step." Instead, I would say, "A journey of a thousand miles begins with a baby step."

I emphasize this because I have seen too many people attempt to take a great leap forward instead of starting with baby steps. We have all seen people who are completely out of shape and suddenly decide to lose 20 pounds. They begin a crash diet, go to the gym for two hours, and then jog 10 miles. This lasts maybe a week. They lose a few pounds, and then the pain, boredom, and hunger begin to wear away at their will power and determination. By the third week, their old habits of overeating, avoiding exercise, and watching television are back in control.

Instead of taking a great leap forward, I strongly recommend taking a baby step forward. Long-term financial success is not measured by how big your stride is, but by the number of steps, the number of years, and the direction in which you're moving. That is the formula for success or failure in any endeavor. When it comes to money, I've seen too many people, myself included, attempt to do too much with too little, and then crash and burn. It's hard to take a baby step forward when you first need a ladder to get yourself out of the financial hole you have dug for yourself.

How Do You Eat an Elephant?

This section of the book describes seven steps to guide you on your path to the right side of the CASHFLOW Quadrant. With the help of my rich dad, I have worked and acted on these steps since I was nine years old, and I will continue to follow them for as long as I live.

For some people, the steps may seem overwhelming—and they will be if you try to do them all in one week. So please begin with baby steps.

We have all heard the saying: "Rome was not built in a day." The saying I use whenever I find myself feeling overwhelmed by how much I have to learn is, "How do you eat an elephant?" The answer is, "One bite at a time." And that is how I recommend you proceed if you find yourself feeling overwhelmed by how much you may have to learn in order to make the journey from the E and S side to the B and I side of the CASHFLOW Quadrant. Please be kind to yourself and realize that the transition is more than just a mental one. It involves emotional learning. After you take baby steps for six months to a year, you're ready to move to walking, and then to running. You've got to walk before you can run. This is the path I recommend. If you don't like this path, then you can do what millions of other people do who want to get rich quickly the fast and easy way, which is to buy a lottery ticket. Who knows? It might be your lucky day.

Action Beats Inaction

To me, one of the primary reasons E's and S's have difficulty moving to the B and I side is because they are too afraid of making mistakes. They often say, "I have a fear of failing," or "I need more information," or "Can you recommend another book?" Their fear or self-doubt is keeping them trapped in their quadrant. I hope that by reading each step, and by completing the action steps that appear at the end of each step in the "Take Action" section, you will keep moving toward the B and I side. Just doing these seven steps will open up whole new worlds of possibility and change. Then just keep taking small baby steps.

Nike's slogan, "Just do it," says it best. Unfortunately, our schools also say, "Don't make mistakes." Millions of highly educated people who want to take action are paralyzed by the emotional fear of making mistakes. One of the most important lessons I have learned as a teacher is that true learning requires mental, emotional, and physical learning. That is why action always beats inaction. If you take action and make a mistake, at least you have learned something, be it mentally, emotionally, or physically. A person who continually searches for the right answer is often afflicted with the disease known as "analysis paralysis," which seems to affect many well-educated people. Ultimately, the way we learn is by making mistakes. We learned to walk and ride a bicycle by falling down and then getting back up. People who are afraid of taking action, out of fear of making mistakes, may be mentally smart, but they are also emotionally and physically handicapped.

A number of years ago, there was a study done of rich and poor all around the world to find out how people born into poverty eventually become wealthy. The study found that these people, regardless of where they live, possess three qualities:

1. They maintain a long-term vision and plan.
2. They believe in delayed gratification.
3. They use the power of compounding in their favor.

The study found that these people thought and planned for the long term and knew that they would ultimately achieve financial success by holding to a dream or a vision. They were willing to make short-term sacrifices to gain long-term success, which is the basis of delayed gratification.

Albert Einstein was amazed at how money could multiply just by the power of compounding. He considered the compounding of money to be one of the most amazing inventions.

This study took compounding beyond money and found that knowledge and learning gained from each baby step also compounded over the years. People who took no steps at all did not have the leverage of a magnified accumulation of knowledge and experience that comes from compounding.

The study also found what caused people to go from wealthy to poor. There are many rich families who lose most of their wealth after only three generations. Not surprisingly, the study found that these people possess the following three qualities:

1. They have short-term vision.
2. They have a desire for immediate gratification.
3. They abuse the power of compounding.

Today I meet people who get frustrated with me because they want me to tell them how they can make more money immediately. They don't like the idea of thinking long-term. Many are desperately seeking short-term answers because they have money problems today caused by consumer debt and lack of investments due to their uncontrolled desire for immediate gratification. They have the idea of, "Eat, drink, and be merry." This abuses the power of compounding and leads to long-term debt instead of long-term wealth.

They want the quick answer. They want me to tell them what to do to acquire great wealth. But they need to understand who they must become first.

In other words, too many people are fixated upon the get-rich-quick philosophy of life. I wish these people luck. They're going to need it.

A Hot Tip

Most of us have heard that people who write down their goals are more likely to achieve them. I have attended many seminars and training sessions on the topic of goal-setting and I learned a concept that I have thought about many times over the years. While it is great to have big long-term dreams and wishes, attaining those dreams is a process made up of many small steps. Instead of trying to be an overachiever, be an underachiever. Be content with small steps, because each one moves you closer to your big goals and dreams.

Even today, I find I achieve more by having an underachiever mindset instead of trying to kill myself and be that overachiever. An example of the way I underachieve is that I set a written goal to listen to two audio tapes a week. I may listen to the same one two or more times if it's good, but it still counts towards my weekly goal.

Kim and I also have a written goal to attend at least two seminars a year on subjects about the B and I quadrants. We go on vacations with people who are experts on subjects found in the B and I quadrants. We learn a lot while playing, resting, and dining out. We achieve more with a lot less stress. Those are ways of underachieving and yet still moving toward big, bold dreams.

The key to making any investment is setting a big goal and approaching it systematically, taking baby steps first and then gradually increasing the size of your investments as your learning and experience increase. You will want to push yourself beyond your comfort zone—but gradually. That is how Kim and I did it. There is nothing wrong with having smaller goals that lead up to the ultimate goal of financial freedom. The same thing applies to getting into good physical shape. I work out with a tough trainer who pushes me to achieve smaller goals on a daily or weekly basis. They increase in intensity as my abilities improve and together they lead up to achieving my big goal.

So dream big daring dreams, and then underachieve a little bit each day. I recommend setting attainable daily goals that, when achieved, provide positive reinforcement to help you stay on the path to the big goal of moving from the left side of the CASHFLOW Quadrant to the right side.

If You Want to Be Rich, You've Got to Change Your Rules

I have often been quoted as saying, "The rules have changed." When people hear these words, they nod their head in agreement and say, "Yes, the rules have changed. Nothing is the same anymore." But then they go on and do the same old thing.

Industrial-Age Financial Statements

When I teach how to get your financial life in order, I start by asking students to fill out a personal financial statement. It often becomes a life-changing experience. Financial statements are much like X-rays. Both let you see what your unassisted eye cannot see. After filling out their statements, it is easy to see who has financial cancer and who is financially healthy. Almost always, the ones with financial cancer are those with Industrial-Age ideas.

Why do I say that? Because in the Industrial Age, people did not have to think about tomorrow. If you worked hard, your employer or the government would take care of all your tomorrows. That is why so many of my friends and family always told me to get a job with the government or to make sure I got a job with an excellent retirement plan. Those are words of advice based on Industrial-Age rules and an entitlement mentality. Although the rules have changed, many people have not changed their financial rules. They are still spending like there's no need to plan for tomorrow. When I read a person's financial statement, it is easy to see what tomorrow might look like for them.

What Does Your Tomorrow Look Like?

Keeping things simple, this is what I look for in a personal financial statement:

INCOME STATEMENT

Income
Expenses *Today*

BALANCE SHEET

Assets	Liabilities
Tomorrow	*Yesterday*

People with no assets that generate cash flow are likely to have tomorrows that are filled with struggles and stress. When I find people who have no assets, they are usually working hard for a paycheck to pay their bills. If you look at most people's expense column, the two biggest monthly expenses are taxes and debt service for long-term liabilities. Their expense statements look like this:

INCOME STATEMENT

Income
Expenses Taxes (approximately 50%) Debt (approximately 35%) Living Expenses

In other words, the government and the bank get paid before they do. People who cannot get control of their cash flow generally have no financial future and will find themselves in serious trouble in the next few years.

Why? A person who only operates in the E quadrant has little protection from taxes and debt. Even an S can do something about these two financial cancers.

If this doesn't make sense to you, I would suggest reading or rereading *Rich Dad Poor Dad,* which should make this and the next few chapters easier to understand.

Three Cash-Flow Patterns

As stated in *Rich Dad Poor Dad,* there are three basic cash-flow patterns: one for the rich, one for the poor, and one for the middle class.

This is the cash-flow pattern of the poor:

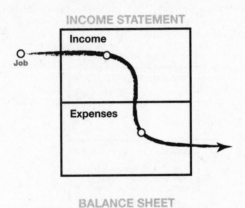

This is the cash-flow pattern of the middle class:

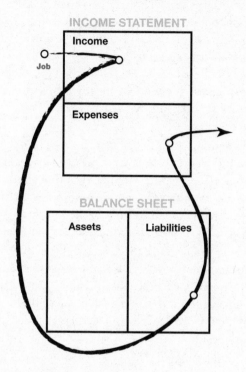

This cash-flow pattern is considered typical and smart by our society. After all, the people who have this pattern probably have high-paying jobs, nice homes, cars, and credit cards. This is what my rich dad called the "working-class dream."

When adults play my *CASHFLOW* board game, they usually struggle mentally. Why? Because they are being introduced to financial literacy, which means understanding the numbers and words of money. The game takes several hours to play, not because it is long, but because the players are learning a completely new subject. It is almost like learning a foreign language. But the good news is that this new literacy can be learned quickly, and then the game picks up speed. The more frequently people play the game, the smarter and faster they get—and they have fun in the process.

Something else also happens. Because they are becoming financially literate, many begin to realize that they are in financial trouble, even though the rest of society thinks they are well-off. A middle-class cash-flow pattern used to work in the Industrial Age, but it could be disastrous in the Information Age.

Many people, once they successfully learn and understand the *CASHFLOW* game, begin to seek new answers. Playing the game becomes a financial wake-up call about their personal financial health, just as a mild heart attack is an alert about a person's physical health.

After playing *CASHFLOW* several times, some people begin to change their thinking pattern to that of the rich.

This is the cash-flow pattern of the rich:

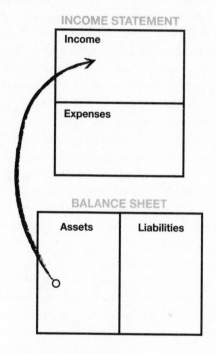

This is the thought pattern rich dad wanted his son and me to have as young children, which is why he took away our paychecks and refused to give us raises. He never wanted us to become addicted to the idea of a high-paying job. He wanted us to develop the thought pattern of thinking only in assets and income in the form of capital gains, dividends, rental income, and residual income from businesses and royalties.

For people who want to be successful in the Information Age, the faster they develop their financial and emotional intelligence, the faster they will feel more financially secure and find financial freedom. In a world of less and less job security, this cash-flow pattern makes much more sense to me. And to achieve this pattern, a person needs to see the world from the B and I quadrants, not from the E and S quadrants.

I also call this an Information-Age financial statement because the income is generated strictly from information, not hard work. In the Information Age, the idea of hard work is not the same as it was in the Agrarian and Industrial Ages. In the Information Age, the people who work the hardest physically will be paid the least. It is already true today and has been true throughout history.

However, today when people say, "Don't work hard. Work smart," they do not mean to work smart in the E or S quadrants. They actually mean to work smart in the B or I quadrants. That is Information-Age thinking, which is why financial and emotional intelligence are vital today and will be even more so in the future.

So What Is the Answer?

Obviously, my answer is to reeducate yourself to think like a rich person. In other words, think and look at the world from the B or I quadrant. However, the solution is not as simple as going back to school and taking a few courses. To be successful in the B or I quadrant requires financial intelligence, systems intelligence, and emotional intelligence. These things cannot be learned in school.

The reason these intelligences are hard to learn is because most adults are wired to the "hard work and spend" mode of life. When they feel financial anxiety, they hurry off to work and work hard. They come home and hear about the stock market going up and down. Their anxiety grows, so they go shopping for a new house or car, or they play golf to avoid the anxiety. The problem is that the anxiety returns on Monday morning.

How Do You Start Thinking Like a Rich Person?

People often ask me how to get started thinking like a rich person. I always recommend starting small and seeking education, rather than running out and jumping into investing. If they are serious about learning and retraining themselves to think like a rich person, I recommend my *CASHFLOW* board game.

I created the game to help teach financial intelligence. It gives people the mental, physical, and emotional training that is required to make the gradual change from thinking like a poor or middle-class person to thinking like a rich person. It teaches people to think about what my rich dad said was important, which is not a large paycheck or a big house, but the accumulation of cash-producing assets.

Cash Flow, Not Money, Relieves Anxiety

Financial struggle and poverty are really financial anxiety problems. There are mental and emotional loops that keep people stuck in, what I call, the Rat Race. Unless the mental and emotional hooks are broken, the pattern remains intact.

I worked with a banker to break his pattern of financial struggle. While I'm certainly not a therapist, I have had experience breaking my own financial habits instilled by my family.

The banker made a good living, but was always in some sort of financial trouble. He had a beautiful family, three cars, a big house, and a vacation home. To the world, he looked like a prosperous banker. But when I looked at his financial statement, I discovered he had a financial cancer that would be terminal in a few years if he did not change his ways.

The first time he and his wife played *CASHFLOW,* he struggled and fidgeted almost uncontrollably. His mind wandered, and he could not seem to grasp the game. After four hours of play, he was still stuck. Everyone else had completed the game, but he was still in the Rat Race.

As we put the game away, I asked him what was going on. His only answer was that the game was too hard, too slow, and too boring. I reminded him about what I had told him before the game started: Games reflect behavior. In other words, a game is like a mirror that allows you to look at yourself.

That statement angered him, so I backed off and asked if he was still committed to getting his financial life in order. He said he was, so I invited him and his wife, who loved the game, to come play again with an investment group I was coaching.

A week later, he reluctantly showed up. This time, a few lights began to go on inside his head. For him, the accounting part was easy, so he was naturally neat and tidy with his numbers, which is important for the game to be valuable. But now he was beginning to understand the world of business and investing. He could finally see with his mind his own life's patterns and what he was doing to cause his own financial struggle. After four hours, he still did not finish the game, but he was beginning to learn. As he left this time, he invited himself back.

By the third meeting, he was a new man. He was now in control of the game, his accounting, and his investments. His confidence soared, and this time he successfully exited the Rat Race and was on the Fast Track. When he left, he purchased a game and said, "I'm going to teach my kids."

By the fourth meeting, he told me his personal expenses were down, he had changed his spending habits and was being more careful with his credit cards, and he was taking an active interest in learning to invest and build his asset column. His thinking was now on track to make him an Information-Age thinker.

At the fifth meeting, he played *CASHFLOW 202*, the advanced game for people who have mastered *CASHFLOW 101*. He was now ready and eager to play the fast and risky game that true B's and I's play. The best news was that he took control of his financial future. This man was completely different from the one who had asked me to make *CASHFLOW* easier the first time he played. A few weeks later, instead of wanting things to be easier, he was actively seeking bigger challenges and was optimistic about his financial future.

He had reeducated himself, not only mentally, but also emotionally, through the power of the repetitive learning process that comes from a game. In my opinion, games are a superior teaching tool because they require the player to become fully engaged in the learning process while having fun. Playing a game involves a person mentally, emotionally, and physically.

THE SEVEN STEPS TO FINDING YOUR FINANCIAL FAST TRACK

Chapter Eleven
STEP 1: IT'S TIME TO MIND YOUR OWN BUSINESS

We are programmed to mind everyone else's business, and ignore our own.

Have you been working hard and making everyone else rich? Starting early in life, most people are programmed to mind other people's businesses and make other people rich. It begins innocently enough with words of advice like these:

- "Go to school and get good grades so you can find a safe, secure job with good pay and excellent benefits."

- "Work hard so you can buy the home of your dreams. After all, your home is an asset and your most important investment."

- "Having a large mortgage is good because the government gives you a tax deduction for your interest payments."

- "Buy now, pay later," or "Low down payment, easy monthly payments," or "Come in and save money."

People who blindly follow these words of advice often become:

1. Employees, making their bosses and owners rich

2. Debtors, making banks and money lenders rich

3. Taxpayers, making the government rich

4. Consumers, making many other businesses rich

Instead of finding their own financial Fast Track, they help everyone else find theirs. Instead of minding their own business, they work all their lives minding everyone else's.

By looking at this financial statement, you can begin to see how we have been programmed from an early age to mind everyone else's business and ignore our own business.

INCOME STATEMENT

Income
You mind your boss's business.

Expenses
You mind the government's business via taxes.
With every other expense, you mind a lot of other people's business.

BALANCE SHEET

Assets	Liabilities
This is your business.	You mind your banker's business.

Take Action

For many people, their financial statements are not a pretty picture, simply because they've been misled into minding everyone else's business instead of minding their own business. To change all that, I suggest following these action steps:

1. **Fill out your own personal financial statement.**

    In order to get where you want to go, you need to know where you are. This is your first step to take control of your life and spend

more time minding your own business.
See the following sample financial statement,
as used in the CASHFLOW game.

2. **Set financial goals.**
   Set a long-term financial goal for where you
   want to be in five years, and a smaller, short-
   term financial goal for where you want to
   be in one year. Set goals that are realistic
   and attainable.

   A. My five-year financial goals are:

   1) I want to increase cash flow (i.e.,
      passive income—income you earn
      without you having to work for it)
      from my assets to $_____per month.

   2) I want to have the following investment
      vehicles in my asset column (e.g.,
      real estate, stocks, businesses,
      commodities)_____

   B. My one-year financial goals are:

   1) I want to decrease my debt by
      $_____.

   2) I want to increase cash flow from my
      assets to $_____per month.

   **C. Using my five-year goals, I will complete
   my financial statement again to show
   how it will look five years from today.**

Now that you know where you are financially today and have set your goals, you need to get control of your cash flow so that you can achieve your goals.

Profession _____ **Player** _____

Goal: Get out of the Rat Race and onto the Fast Track by building up your **Passive Income** to be **greater** than your **Total Expenses**

INCOME STATEMENT

INCOME

Description	Cash Flow
Salary:	
Interest/Dividends:	
Real Estate/Business:	

Auditor _____
(Person on your right)

Passive Income : $ _____
(Cash Flow from
Interest/Dividends +
Real Estate/Business)

**Total
Income:** $ _____

EXPENSES

Taxes:	
Home Mortgage Payment:	
School Loan Payment:	
Car Loan Payment:	
Credit Card Payment:	
Retail Payment:	
Other Expenses:	
Child Expenses:	
Loan Payment:	

Number of
Children: _____
(Begin game with 0 Children)

Per Child
Expense: $ _____

**Total
Expenses:** $ _____

BALANCE SHEET

Monthly Cash Flow (PAYCHECK): $ _____
(Total Income - Total Expenses)

ASSETS

Savings:		
Stocks/Funds/CDs:	# of Shares:	Cost/Share:
Real Estate/Business:	Down Pay:	Cost:

LIABILITIES

Home Mortgage:	
School Loans:	
Car Loans:	
Credit Cards:	
Retail Debt:	
Real Estate/Business:	Mortgage/Liability:
Loan:	

313

Chapter Twelve
STEP 2: TAKE CONTROL OF YOUR CASH FLOW

People who cannot control their cash flow work for those who can.

Many people believe that simply making more money will solve their money problems. But, in most cases, it only causes bigger ones.

The primary reason most people have money problems is that they were never schooled in the science of cash-flow management. They were taught how to read, write, drive cars, and swim, but not how to manage their cash flow. Without this training, they wind up having money problems and then work harder with the belief that more money will solve the problem.

As my rich dad often said, "More money will not solve the problem if cash-flow management is the problem."

The Most Important Skill

After your commitment to mind your own business, the next step as the CEO of the business of your life is to take control of your cash flow. If you do not, making more money will not make you richer. In fact, more money makes most people poorer because they often increase their spending and get deeper into debt every time they get a pay raise.

Who Is Smarter—You or Your Banker?

The majority of people do not prepare personal financial statements. At most, they try to balance their checkbooks each month. So congratulate yourself, because you're already ahead of most of your colleagues, simply by completing your financial statement and setting goals for yourself. As CEO of your life, you can learn to be smarter than most people, even your banker.

Most people believe that keeping two sets of books is illegal, and that is true in some instances. But if you truly understand the world of finances, there must always be two sets of books. Once you realize this, you will be as smart, and maybe smarter, than your banker.

As CEO of your life, always remember these simple words and diagrams from my rich dad, who often said, "For every liability you have, you are somebody else's asset."

The following is an example of two sets of books—yours, and your banker's:

YOUR BALANCE SHEET

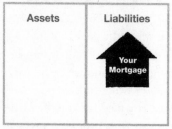

BANK'S BALANCE SHEET

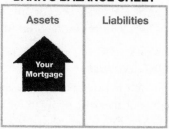

As CEO of your life, you must always remember that, for each of your liabilities or debts, you are someone else's asset. That is the real two-sets-of-books accounting. For every liability, such as a mortgage, car loan, school loan, and credit card, you are an employee of the people lending the money. You're working hard to make someone else rich.

Good Debt and Bad Debt

Rich dad often cautioned me about good debt and bad debt. He would often say, "Every time you owe someone money, you become an employee of their money. If you take out a 30-year loan, you've become a 30-year employee, and they do not give you a gold watch when the debt is retired."

Rich dad did borrow money, but he did his best to not become the person who paid for his loans. He would explain to Mike and me that good debt was debt someone else paid for you. Bad debt was debt that you paid for with your own sweat and blood. That is why he loved rental properties. He encouraged me to buy rental real estate because "the bank gives you the loan, but your tenant pays for it."

Income and Expense

Not only do the two sets of books apply to assets and liabilities, but they also apply to income and expenses. The more complete verbal lesson from my rich dad was this: "For most every liability, there must be an asset, but they don't appear on the same set of financial statements. For every expense, there must also be income, and again, they do not appear on the same set of financial statements."

This simple drawing will make that lesson clearer:

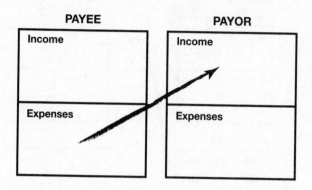

The Financial Fast Track and the Rat Race

The concept of two sets of books can be used to show you the financial Fast Track and the Rat Race. There are many different types of financial Fast Tracks. The diagram below is one of the most common. It is the track between a creditor and a debtor.

It is simplified but, if you take the time to study it, your mind will begin to see what most people's eyes do not. You will see the relationship between the rich and the poor, the haves and have-nots, the borrowers and lenders, those who create jobs and those who look for jobs.

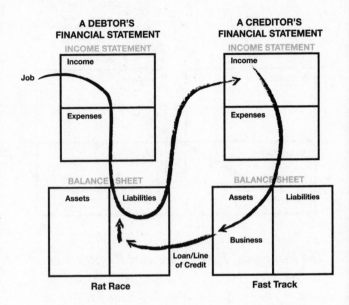

The creditor will often say, "Because of your good credit, we'd like to offer you a bill-consolidation loan," or "Would you like to open a line of credit just in case you need some extra money in the future?"

Do You Know the Difference?

The path of money flowing between the two sets of books is what rich dad called the financial Fast Track and the financial Rat Race. For one to exist, so must the other. Hence, there must be at minimum two financial statements. The questions are: Which statement is yours? Which statement do you want to have?

This is why rich dad constantly told me, "Making more money will not solve your problems if cash-flow management is the problem. The people who understand the power of financial numbers have power over those who do not."

That is why Step 2 to finding your own financial Fast Track is: "Take control of your cash flow."

You need to sit down and map out a plan to get control of your spending and minimize your debt and liabilities. Live within your means, before you start to expand your means.

Take Action

1. **Review your financial statements from Step 1.**

2. **Determine which quadrant of the CASHFLOW Quadrant you receive your income from today.**_____

3. **Determine which quadrant you want to receive the bulk of your income from in five years.** _____

4. **Begin your Cash-Flow Management Plan:**

   A. **Pay yourself first.**

      Put aside a set percentage from each paycheck or each payment you receive from other sources. Deposit that money into an investment savings account.

Once your money goes into the account, NEVER take it out until you are ready to invest it.

Congratulations! You have just started managing your cash flow.

B. Focus on reducing your personal consumer debt.

The following are some simple tips for reducing and eliminating personal debt.

Tip #1

If you have credit cards with outstanding balances, discipline yourself to use only one or two credit cards. Any new charges must be paid off in full every month. Do not incur any more long-term debt.

Tip #2

Come up with $150–$200 extra per month. Now that you are becoming more and more financially literate, this should be relatively easy to do. If you cannot generate an additional $150–$200 per month, then your chances for financial freedom may only be a pipe dream.

Tip #3

Apply the additional $150–$200 to your monthly payment of ONLY ONE of your credit cards. You will now pay the minimum PLUS the $150–$200 on that one credit card.

Pay only the minimum amount due on all other credit cards. Often people try to pay a little extra each month on all their cards, but those cards surprisingly never get paid off.

Tip #4
Once the first card is paid off, apply the total amount you were paying each month on that card to your next credit card. You are now paying the minimum amount due on the second card PLUS the total monthly payment you were paying on your first credit card.

Continue this process with all your credit cards and other consumer-credit debt. With each debt you pay off, apply the full amount you were paying on that debt to the minimum payment of your next debt. As you pay off each debt, the monthly amount you are paying on the next debt will escalate.

Tip #5
Once all your credit cards and other consumer debt is paid off, continue the procedure with your car and house payments. If you follow this procedure, you will be amazed at the shortened amount of time it takes for you to be completely debt-free. Most people can be debt-free within five to seven years.

Tip #6
Now that you are completely debt-free, take the monthly amount you were paying on your last debt, and put that money toward investments. Build your asset column.

That's how simple it is.

STEP 3: **KNOW THE DIFFERENCE BETWEEN RISK AND RISKY**

Business and investing are not risky,
but being under-educated is.

What Is Proper Cash-Flow Management?

Proper cash-flow management begins with really knowing the difference between an asset and a liability. The following diagram shows the properly managed cash flow of an individual who is 45 years old:

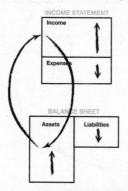

I use the age 45 because it is halfway between 25, the age when most people begin to work, and 65, the age when most people plan on retiring. By age 45, if a person has managed their cash flow properly, their asset column should be longer than their liability column.

This is a person who takes risks, but not excessive risk, and is in the upper 10 percent of the population. But if they do what the other 90 percent of the population does, which is mismanage their cash flow and not know the difference between an asset and a liability, then at age 45, their financial picture looks like this:

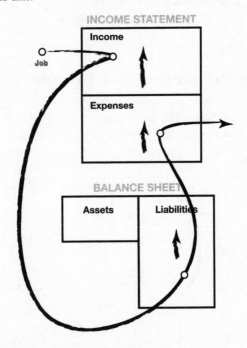

These are the people who most often say, "Investing is risky." For them, it is risky, but not because investing is risky. It is their lack of knowledge and formal financial training that makes investing risky.

Financial Literacy

In *Rich Dad Poor Dad,* I explained that my rich dad demanded that I become financially literate.

Financial literacy is not simply looking at the numbers with your eyes, but also training your mind to tell you which way the cash is flowing. Rich dad often said, "The direction of cash flow is everything."

So a house could be an asset or a liability depending on the direction of the cash flow. If the cash flows into your pocket, it is an asset. If it flows out of your pocket, it is a liability.

Financial Intelligence

Rich dad had many definitions for financial intelligence, such as "the ability to convert cash or labor into assets that provide cash flow." But one of his favorite sayings was, "Who is smarter? You, or your money?"

For rich dad, spending your life working hard for money only to have it go out as fast as it comes in is not a sign of high intelligence. You may want to review the cash-flow patterns of a poor person, a middle-class person, and a rich person presented in chapter ten. Remember that a rich person focuses his or her efforts on acquiring assets, not working harder.

Due to their lack of financial intelligence, many educated people put themselves into positions of high financial risk. My rich dad called it "the financial red line," meaning income and expenses are nearly the same every month. These are the people who cling desperately to job security, are unable to change when the economy changes, and often destroy their health with stress and worry. And these are often the same people who say, "Business and investing are risky."

In my opinion, business and investing are not risky, but being under-educated is. Similarly, being misinformed is risky, and relying on a safe, secure job is the highest risk anyone can take. Buying an asset is not risky. Buying liabilities you have been told are assets is risky. Minding your own business is not risky. Minding everyone else's business and paying them first is risky.

So Step 3 is to know the difference between risk and risky.

Take Action

1. **Define risk in your own words.**

   A. Is relying on a paycheck risky to you?

   B. Is having debt to pay each month risky to you?

   C. Is owning an asset that generates cash flow each month risky to you?

   D. Is spending time to obtain financial education risky to you?

   E. Is spending time learning about different types of investments risky to you?

2. **Commit five hours of your time each week to do one or more of the following:**

   A. Read the business section of your newspaper and the *Wall Street Journal.*

   B. Listen to the financial news on television or radio.

   C. Read financial websites, magazines, and newsletters.

   D. Play the *CASHFLOW* game, and visit a local CASHFLOW Club.

   E. Attend educational seminars on investing and financial education.

   F. Consider hiring a coach to help you work through the process of becoming financially free.

Chapter Fourteen
STEP 4: **DECIDE WHAT KIND OF INVESTOR YOU WANT TO BE**

Start small, and learn to solve problems.

Have you ever wondered why some investors make more money with a lot less risk than others?

Most people struggle financially because they avoid financial problems. One of the biggest secrets my rich dad taught me was this: If you want to acquire great wealth quickly, take on great financial problems.

In Part I of this book, I discussed the five levels of investors. I would like to add one more distinction that defines three different types of investors:

- Type A: Investors who seek problems.

- Type B: Investors who seek answers.

- Type C: Investors who seek an "expert" to tell them what to do.

Type-C Investors

Type-C investors are financially uneducated and look for people to tell them what to invest in. People in the E and S quadrants have been forced into the investing game because of changes in retirement plans. They have little interest in investing in their education so they can become better investors. They know nothing, which means they have to rely on the advice of other so-called experts.

What's the chance of the Type-C investor getting rich? About as much chance as winning the lottery.

Type-B Investors

Type-B investors seek answers. They often ask questions like:

- "What do you recommend I invest in?"

- "Do you think I should buy real estate?"

- "What stocks are good for me?

- "I talked to my broker, and he recommended I diversify."

- "My parents gave me a few shares of stock. Should I sell them?"

Type-B investors should interview several tax advisors, attorneys, stock brokers and real estate agents, choose carefully and start implementing their advice. They should find advisors who practice what they preach and run fast from anyone who is selling investment advice and getting rich on commissions and fees alone. Type-B investors should look for investment advisors who make money investing in the same investments they are selling.

I often find that many high-income E's and S's fall into the Type-B investor category because they are busy and have little time to look for investment opportunities or learn about the right side of the CASHFLOW Quadrant. Hence, they want somebody to give them the answers instead of gaining knowledge for themselves. This group often buys what the Type-A investor calls "retail investments," which are investments that have been packaged for sale to the masses.

Type-A Investors

Type-A investors look for problems. In particular, they look for problems caused by those who get into financial trouble. Investors who are good at solving problems expect to make returns of 25 percent to infinity on their money. They are typically Level-5 investors with strong financial foundations. They possess the skills necessary to succeed as business owners and investors, and they use those skills to solve problems caused by people who lack such skills.

For example, when I first started investing with only $18,000, I focused on small condominiums and houses that were in foreclosure because of problems created by investors who did not manage their cash flow well and ran out of money.

After a few years, I was still looking for problems, but this time, the numbers were bigger. Several years ago, I was working on acquiring a $30 million mining company in Peru. While the problem and numbers were bigger, the process was the same.

How to Get on the Fast Track Faster

If you start small and learn to solve problems, you will gain immense wealth as you become better and better at solving problems.

For those who wish to acquire assets faster, I again emphasize the need to first learn the skills of the B and I quadrants. I recommend learning how to build a business first because it provides vital educational experience, improves personal skills, provides cash flow to soften the ups and downs of the marketplace, and provides free time. It is the cash flow from my business that bought me the free time to begin looking for financial problems to solve.

Can You Be All Three Types of Investors?

In reality, I operate as all three types of investors. I am a Type-C investor when it comes to mutual funds. When I am asked, "What mutual funds do you recommend?" I tell the person, "I have no idea."

As a Type-B investor, I seek professional answers to my financial problems. I seek answers from my advisors, including tax and wealth strategists, stockbrokers, bankers, and real estate brokers. When you find good ones, these professionals provide a wealth of information many people do not personally have the time to acquire.

The advice from my financial advisors is valuable because they know trusts, wills, and insurance far better than I ever will. They are also closer to the market and more up-to-date with any changes in the laws and how that might affect the markets. There is much more to investing than simply buying and selling.

I also give my money to other investors to invest for me. In other words, I partner with other Level-4 and Level-5 investors in their investments. These are individuals I personally know and trust. If they choose to invest in an area I know nothing about, such as low-income housing or large office buildings, I may choose to give my money to them because I know they are good at what they do and I trust their knowledge.

Why You Should Get Started Quickly

One of the main reasons I recommend that people find their own financial Fast Track quickly and take getting rich seriously is because, in America and most of the world, there are two sets of rules: one for the rich, and one for everyone else. Many laws are written against people stuck in the financial Rat Race. In the world of business and investing, I find it shocking how little the middle class knows when it comes to where its tax dollars are going. Although tax dollars are going to many worthwhile causes, many of the larger tax breaks, incentives, and payments are going to the rich. And the middle class pays for them.

For example, insufficient low-income housing in America is a huge problem and a political hot potato.

To help solve this problem, cities, states, and the federal government offer substantial tax credits, tax breaks, and subsidized rents to people who finance and build low-income housing. Just by knowing the laws, financiers and builders become wealthier by having taxpayers subsidize their investments in low-income housing.

Why It's Unfair

Not only do most people on the left side of the CASHFLOW Quadrant pay more in personal income tax, but they are also often unable to participate in tax-advantaged investments. This may be another reason why the rich get richer.

I know it's unfair, and I understand both sides of the story. I have met people who protest and write letters to the editor of their newspapers or try to change the system by running for political office. I say it is much easier to simply mind your own business, take control of your cash flow, find your own financial Fast Track, and get rich. It is easier to change yourself than to change the political system.

Problems Lead to Opportunities

Years ago, rich dad encouraged me to develop my skills as a business owner and investor and then practice solving problems.

For years, that is all I have done. I solve business and investment problems. Some people prefer to call them challenges, but I like to call them problems because that is what they are, for the most part.

I think people like the word "challenges" more than "problems" because they think one word sounds more positive than the other. But I think that the word "problem" has a positive meaning. I know that inside every problem lies an opportunity, and opportunities are what real investors are after. And with every financial or business problem I address, regardless of whether I solve the problem or not, I wind up learning something new about finance, marketing, people, or legal affairs. I often meet new people who become invaluable assets on other projects. Many have become lifelong friends, which is a priceless bonus.

Find Your Fast Track

So for those of you who want to find your financial Fast Track, start by:

1. Minding your own business

2. Taking control of your cash flow

3. Knowing the difference between risk and risky

4. Knowing the difference between a Type A, B, and C investor

To get on the financial Fast Track, become an expert at solving a certain type of problem. Do not diversify like Type-B investors are advised to do. Become an expert at solving one type of problem, and people will come to you with money to invest. Then, if you're good and trustworthy, you will reach your financial Fast Track more quickly.

Here are a few examples: Bill Gates is an expert at solving software-marketing problems, Donald Trump is an expert at solving problems in real estate, and Warren Buffett is an expert at solving problems in business and the stock market, which in turn allows him to buy valuable stocks and manage a successful portfolio. George Soros is an expert at solving problems resulting from market volatility which makes him an excellent hedge-fund manager. Rupert Murdock is an expert at solving the business problems of global television networks.

Kim and I are Type-A investors and solve problems in apartment housing. That has paid off with a generous and steady flow of passive income. If we choose to invest in areas outside the multi-family housing market, we become Type-B investors, which means we give our money to people who have an excellent track record in their fields of expertise and who practice what they preach.

I have one focused objective, and that is to mind my own business. Although Kim and I do work for charities and help other people in their efforts, we never lose sight of the importance of minding our own business and continually adding to our asset column.

So to become rich quicker, become a student of the skills needed by a business owner and investor. Seek to solve bigger problems, because inside big problems lie huge financial opportunities. That is why I recommend becoming a B first, before becoming an I. If you master solving business problems, you will have excess cash flow, and your knowledge of business will make you a much smarter investor. I have said it many times before, but it is worth saying again: Many people come to the I quadrant hoping that investing will solve their financial problems. In most cases, it does not. Investing only makes their financial problems worse if they are not already sound business owners.

There is no scarcity of financial problems. In fact, there is one right around the corner from you, waiting to be solved.

Take Action

1. **Get educated in investing.**
   Once again, I recommend you become proficient as a Level-4 investor before trying to become a Level-5 investor. Start small, and continue your education.

   Each week do at least two of the following:

   A. Attend financial seminars and classes. I attribute much of my success to a real estate course I took as a young man that cost me $385. It has earned me millions over the years because I took action.

   B. Look for For-Sale signs in your area. Call on three or four per week and ask the agent to tell you about the property. Ask questions like: Is it an investment property? Is it rented? What is the current rent? What is the vacancy rate? What are the average rents in that area? What are the maintenance costs? Is there deferred maintenance? Will the owner finance? What types of financing terms are available?

Practice calculating the monthly cash-flow statement for each property and then go over it with the real estate agent to see what you forgot. Each property is a unique business system and should be viewed as an individual business system.

C. Meet with several stockbrokers and listen to the companies they recommend for stock buys. Research those companies and consider opening a trading account and making some small investments.

D. Subscribe to investment newsletters and study them.

E. Continue to read, attend seminars, watch financial TV programs, and play *CASHFLOW.*

2. **Get educated in business.**

    A. Meet with several business brokers to see what existing businesses are for sale in your area. It is amazing how much terminology you can learn by just asking questions and listening.

    B. Attend a network-marketing seminar to learn about its business system. (I recommend researching at least three different network-marketing companies.)

    C. Attend business-opportunity conventions or trade expos in your area to see what franchises or business systems are available.

    D. Subscribe to business newspapers, magazines, and other types of communications.

Chapter Fifteen
STEP 5: **SEEK MENTORS**

---

*A mentor is someone who tells you what is important
and what is not important.*

Who guides you to places you have never been
to before? A mentor is someone who tells you what is
important and what is not important.

Mentors Tell Us What Is Important

The following financial statement from the
CASHFLOW board game was created to be a mentor.
It trains people to think like my rich dad thought and
points out what he considered to be financially important.

My highly educated, but poor, dad thought that a
job with a high salary was important and that buying
your dream home was important. He also believed in
paying bills first and living below your means.

My rich dad taught me to focus on passive income
and spend my time acquiring assets that provide passive
or long-term residual income. He did not believe in
living below your means. To his son and me, he often
said, "Instead of living below your means, focus on
expanding your means."

To do that, he recommended that we focus on building the asset column and increasing our passive income from capital gains, dividends, residual income from businesses, rental income from real estate, and royalties.

Both dads served as strong mentors for me as I grew up. The fact that I chose to follow the financial advice of my rich dad did not lessen the impact that my poor dad had on me. I would not be who I am today without the strong influence of both of these men.

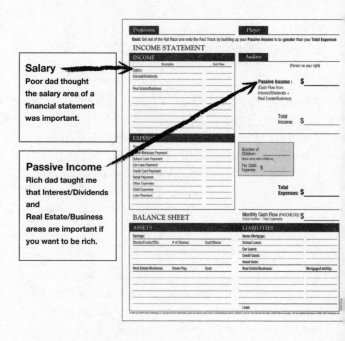

Salary
Poor dad thought the salary area of a financial statement was important.

Passive Income
Rich dad taught me that Interest/Dividends and Real Estate/Business areas are important if you want to be rich.

Reverse Role Models

Just as there are mentors who are excellent role models, there are people who are bad role models. In most instances, we all have both types in our lives.

For example, I have a friend who has made more than $800 million in his lifetime, but today he's bankrupt. I have had other friends ask me why I continue to spend time with him. The answer to that question is because he is both an excellent role model and an excellent reverse role model. I can learn from both role models. One teaches me what to do, while the other serves as an example of what not to do.

Spiritual Role Models

Both of my dads were spiritual men, but when it came to money and spirituality, they had different points of view. For instance, they interpreted the meaning behind, "The love of money is the root of all evil" differently.

My highly educated but poor dad felt any desire to have more money or to improve your financial position was wrong.

On the other hand, rich dad believed that temptation, greed, and financial ignorance were wrong. In other words, rich dad did not think money by itself was evil. He did believe that working all your life as a slave to money was evil, and to be in financial slavery to personal debt was evil.

My rich dad often had a way of converting religious teachings into financial lessons, and I would like to share one of those lessons with you now.

The Power of Temptation

Rich dad believed that individuals who worked hard, were chronically in debt, and lived beyond their means were poor role models for their children because they gave into temptation and greed.

He would often draw a diagram like the following and say, "And lead us not into temptation," as he pointed to the liability column.

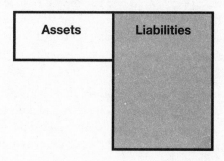

Rich dad believed that many financial problems came from the desire to possess items that had little value. When credit cards arrived, he foresaw that millions of people would go into debt which would eventually control their lives. We see people going into tremendous personal debt for homes, furnishings, clothes, vacations, and cars because they lack control over that human emotion called temptation. Today, people work harder and harder to buy things they think are assets, but their spending habits will never allow them to acquire real assets.

Rich dad would then point to the asset column and say, "But deliver us from evil."

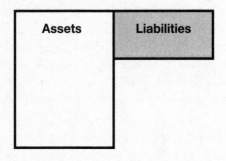

This was rich dad's way of saying that delaying gratification (a sign of emotional intelligence), minding your own business, and building your asset column first would help you avoid the degradation of the human spirit caused by temptation, lack of financial education, and the influence of financially poor role models.

For those of you seeking your own personal Fast Track, I can only caution you to be careful about the people you surround yourself with. Ask yourself: Are they good role models? If not, I suggest you spend more time with people who are heading in the same direction you are.

If you cannot find them at work, look for them in investment clubs, network-marketing groups, and other business associations.

Find Someone Who's Been There

Choose your mentors wisely. Be careful from whom you take advice. If you want to go somewhere, it is best to find someone who has already taken the journey.

For example, if you decide to climb Mount Everest next year, obviously you would seek advice from someone who had climbed the mountain before. However, when it comes to climbing financial mountains, most people get advice from people who are stuck in financial swamps.

It is hard to find mentors who are B's and I's. Most people giving advice about those quadrants and about money are people who actually come from the E and S quadrants.

Rich dad encouraged me to always have a coach or mentor. He constantly said, "Professionals have coaches. Amateurs do not."

For example, I play golf and I take lessons, but I do not have a full-time golf coach. This is probably why I pay money to play golf instead of getting paid to play. But when it comes to the game of business and investing, I do have coaches, several of them. Why? Because I get paid to play those games.

So choose your teachers and mentors wisely. It is one of the most important things you can do.

Take Action

1. **Seek mentors.**
   Find individuals in both the investment and business arenas who might act as mentors to you.

   A. Seek out role models. Learn from them.

   B. Seek out reverse role models. Learn from them.

2. **Who you spend your time with is your future. Write down the six people you spend the most time with.**
   Remember that the qualifier is who you spend the most time with, not the nature of your relationship. (All of your children count as one person.) *Don't read any further until you have written down your six names.*

   I was at a seminar many years ago when the instructor asked us to do this. He then asked us to examine the names we had written and announced, "You are looking at your future. The six people you spend the most time with are your future."

   These six people you spend the most time with may not always be personal friends. They may be your co-workers, spouse, children, or members of your church or other social groups. My list consisted of co-workers, business associates, and rugby players. It was pretty revealing once I began to look below the surface.

I gained insights about myself that I liked, and even more that I didn't.

The instructor had us go around the room and discuss our lists with others. After a while, the relevance of the exercise began to sink in even deeper. The more I discussed my list with other people and the more I listened to them, the more I realized that I needed to make some changes. This exercise had little to do with the people I was spending my time with, and everything to do with where I was going and what I was doing with my life.

Today, the people I spend the most time with are all different except one. The five others on my earlier list are still dear friends, but we rarely see each other. They are great people, and they are happy with their lives. Their removal from my list was all about me. I wanted to change my future. To do that, I had to change my thoughts, and the people I spent time with.

3. **In your list of six people, after each person's name, list the quadrant they operate from. Are they an E, S, B, or I?**

   If they are unemployed or retired, list the quadrant they earned their income from when they worked. Leave a blank for young children and students. *A reminder: The quadrant reflects the way that person generates the majority of their income.*

A person can have more than one designation. For example, my wife Kim would have a B and an I next to her name since she generates income from each.

My list would have Kim at the top since she and I spend almost all of our time together.

NAME	QUADRANT(S)
1. *Kim Kiyosaki*	*B, I*
2.	
3.	
4.	
5.	
6.	

4. **The next step is to list each person's level as an investor.**
   Please refer to chapter five and the "Five Levels of Investors." Kim is a Level-5 investor. If you do not know a person's investor level, do your best and take an educated guess.

NAME	QUADRANT(S)	INVESTOR LEVEL
1. *Kim Kiyosaki*	*B, I*	*Level 5*
2.		
3.		
4.		
5.		
6.		

I have had mixed reviews from people about this exercise. Some people get very angry. I have been told, "How dare you ask me to classify the people around me!" So if this exercise has caused any emotional upset, please accept my apologies. It is not intended to upset anyone but is designed to shine some light on an individual's life. It does for some, but not for everyone.

When I did this exercise years ago, I realized that I was playing it safe and hiding. I was not happy where I was, and I used the people I worked with as the excuse for why I was not making progress in my life. There were two people in particular with whom I argued constantly, blaming them for holding our company back. My daily routine at work was to find their faults, point those flaws out to them, and then blame them for the problems we had as an organization.

After completing this exercise, I realized that the two people I was always bumping heads with were very happy where they were. I was the one who wanted to change. Instead of changing myself, I was pressuring them to change. After doing this exercise, I realized that I was projecting my personal expectations onto others. I wanted them to do what I did not want to do. I thought they should want and have the same things I did. Clearly, they were not healthy relationships. Once I realized this, I was able to take steps to change myself.

5. **Take a look at the CASHFLOW Quadrant and place the initials of the people you spend time with in the appropriate quadrant.**

   Then put your initials in the quadrant you are in at present.

   Next, put your initials in the quadrant you want to operate from in the future.

   If the initials are all primarily in the same quadrant, chances are you are a happy person because you are surrounded by like-minded people. If they are not all in the same quadrant, you may want to consider some changes in your life.

Chapter Sixteen
STEP 6: MAKE DISAPPOINTMENT YOUR STRENGTH

*Inside every disappointment
lies a priceless gem of wisdom.*

When I left the Marine Corps, rich dad recommended that I get a job that taught me how to sell. He knew I was shy and that learning to sell was the last thing in the world I wanted to do.

For two years, I was the worst salesman in my company. I could not sell a life preserver to a drowning man. My shyness was painful, not only for me, but also to the customers I was trying to sell to. For those two years, I was often on probation and always on the verge of being fired.

I often blamed the economy, the product I was trying to sell, or even the customers for my lack of success. But rich dad told me, "When people are lame, they love to blame."

He meant that the emotional pain from the disappointment is so strong that a person pushes the pain onto someone else through blame. In order to learn to sell, I had to face the pain of disappointment. But in the process of learning to sell, I found a priceless lesson: how to turn disappointment into an asset rather than a liability.

Whenever I meet people who are afraid to try something new, in most cases the reason lies in their fear of being disappointed. They are afraid they might make a mistake or get rejected. If you are ready to start your journey to the financial Fast Track, I offer you the same words of advice and encouragement that rich dad offered me when I was learning something new: Be prepared to be disappointed.

He meant this in a positive, not negative, sense. He believed that if you are prepared for disappointment, you can turn that disappointment into an asset. Most people turn disappointment into a liability, a long-term one. You notice this when they say, "I'll never do that again," or "I should have known I would fail."

Just as inside every problem lies an opportunity, inside every disappointment lies a priceless gem of wisdom.

Whenever I hear someone say, "I'll never do that again," I know I am listening to someone who has stopped learning. They are letting disappointment stop them. Disappointment has erected a protective wall around them, instead of a foundation from which to grow.

Rich dad helped me learn how to deal with deep emotional disappointments. He would say, "The reason there are few self-made rich people is because few people can tolerate disappointment. Instead of learning to face disappointment, they spend their lives avoiding it."

Rich dad believed that disappointment is an important part of learning. Just as we learn from our mistakes, we gain character from our disappointments. The following are some words of advice he gave me over the years:

- **_Expect to be disappointed._**
  Rich dad often said, "Only fools expect everything to go the way they want. Expecting to be disappointed does not mean being passive or a defeated loser. Expecting to be disappointed is a way of mentally and emotionally preparing yourself to be ready for surprises that you may not want. By being emotionally prepared, you can be calm and dignified when things do not go your way. When you are calm, you think better."

  Over the years, I have met many people with great new business ideas. Their excitement lasts about a month, and then disappointment begins to wear them down. Soon their excitement is diminished, and all you hear them say is, "That was a good idea, but it didn't work."

It's not the idea that didn't work. It was disappointment that worked harder. They allowed their impatience to turn into disappointment, and then they allowed the disappointment to defeat them. Many times this impatience is because they did not receive immediate financial reward. Business owners and investors may wait years to see cash flow from a business or investment, but they go into it with the knowledge that success may take time. They also know that when success is achieved, the financial reward will be well worth the wait.

- *Have a mentor standing by.*
  Like those emergency numbers for fire and police that we always have handy, who is on your list of trusted and knowledgeable contacts? For me, my financial mentors take center stage. They are only a phone call away if I have a financial emergency.

  Often, before I go into a deal or venture, I call one of my friends and explain what I'm doing and what I intend to accomplish. I also ask them to stand by in case I find myself in over my head, which is often.

  I was once negotiating for a large piece of real estate with a seller who was playing hardball and changing the terms at the closing. He knew I wanted the property, and he was doing his best to get more money from me at the last minute. Having a hot temper, my emotions went out of control. But instead of blowing the deal by yelling and shouting, which is my normal inclination, I simply asked if I could use the phone to call my partner.

I talked to my three friends who were standing by. After getting their advice on how to handle the situation, I calmed down and learned three new ways to negotiate that I had not known before. The deal never went through, but I still use those negotiation techniques today— techniques I would never have learned if I had not tried to do the deal. That knowledge is priceless.

The point is that we can never know everything beforehand, and we often only learn things when we need to learn them. That is why I recommend that you try new things and expect disappointment, but always have a mentor standing by to coach you through the experience. Many people never start projects simply because they don't have all the answers. You will never have all the answers, but begin anyway. One of my friends always says, "Many people will not head down the street until all the lights are green. That is why they don't go anywhere."

- ***Be kind to yourself.***

  One of the most painful aspects about making a mistake or failing at something is not what other people say about us, but how hard we are on ourselves. Most people who make a mistake beat themselves up far more than anyone else would.

  I have found that people who are hard on themselves mentally and emotionally are often too cautious when it comes to taking risks, adopting new ideas, or attempting something new. It is hard to learn anything new if you punish yourself for your personal disappointments.

- ***Tell the truth.***

  One of the worst punishments I ever received as a child was the day I accidentally broke my sister's front tooth. She ran home to tell my dad, and I ran to hide.

  After my father found me, he was very angry. He scolded me, "The reason I'm punishing you isn't because you broke your sister's tooth, but because you ran away."

  Financially, there have been many times I could have run from my mistakes, but running away is taking the easy way out.

  In short, we all make mistakes. We all feel upset and disappointed when things don't go our way. The difference lies in how we process that disappointment. Rich dad said, "The size of your success is measured by the strength of your desire, the size of your dream, and how you handle disappointment along the way."

In the next few years, we will have financial changes that will test our courage. As Bob Dylan sang, "The times they are a-changin'." The people who are most in control of their emotions, who do not let their emotions hold them back, and who have the emotional maturity to learn new financial skills will flourish in the years ahead.

The future belongs to those who can change with the times and use personal disappointments as building blocks for the future.

Take Action

1. **Make mistakes.**

   That is why I recommend starting with baby steps. Remember that losing is part of winning. E's and S's are trained to think that making mistakes is not acceptable. B's and I's know that making mistakes is how they learn.

2. **Start small.**

   If you find an investment you want to invest in, put a little money down. It is amazing how quickly your intelligence grows when you have money on the line. Don't bet the ranch, your mortgage payment, or your retirement. Simply put a little money down, pay attention, and learn.

3. **The key is to TAKE ACTION!**

   Reading, watching, and listening are all crucial to your education. But you must also start DOING. Make offers on small real estate deals that will generate positive cash flow, join a network-marketing company and learn about it from the inside, invest in stock after researching the company. Seek advice from your mentor or financial or tax advisor if you need it. As Nike says, "Just Do It!"

Chapter Seventeen
STEP 7: **THE POWER OF FAITH**

---

*The only person who determines the thoughts
you choose to believe about yourself, is you.*

In my senior year of high school, rich dad's son
Mike and I were lined up in front of a small group
of students made up primarily of the leaders of our
class. Our guidance counselor turned to Mike and
me and declared, "The two of you will never amount
to anything." Some of our classmates laughed as the
counselor continued, "From now on, I am not going to
waste any more time on either of you. I am only going
to spend my time with these students who are the class
leaders. You two are the class clowns with bad grades,
and you will never amount to anything. Now get out
of here."

Biggest Favor of All

That counselor did Mike and me a huge favor.
While her words hurt us deeply, they also inspired
both of us to strive even harder. Her words carried us
through college and into our own businesses.

High School Reunion

A few years ago, Mike and I went to our high school reunion, always an interesting experience. It was nice to visit with people we had spent three years with during a period of time when none of us really knew who we were. It was also interesting to see that most of the so-called senior leaders had not become successful in the years after high school.

Mike and I were not academic whiz kids. We were not class leaders, financial geniuses, or athletic stars. For the most part, we were slow to average learners and students. In my opinion, we were not as naturally gifted as our fathers. But it was those stinging words from that guidance counselor, coupled with the snickering from our classmates, that gave us the fire to plod along, to learn from our mistakes, and to keep going in both good times and bad times.

Just because you did not do well in school, were not popular, are not good in math, are rich or poor, or have other reasons to sell yourself short—none of it matters in the long run. Those so-called shortcomings only count if you think they count.

For those of you who are considering embarking on your own financial Fast Track, you may have some doubts about your abilities. All I can say is: Trust that you have everything you need right now to be successful financially. All it takes to bring out your natural, God-given gifts is your desire, determination, and a deep faith that you have a genius and a gift that is unique.

Look in the Mirror and Listen to the Words

A mirror reflects back more than just a visual image. It often reflects back our thoughts. How often have we seen people look in the mirror and say such things as:

- "Oh, I look horrible."
- "Have I put on that much weight?"
- "I'm really getting old."

or

- "My, my, my! I am damned good-looking. I am God's gift to women."

Thoughts Are Reflections

Mirrors reflect back much more than just what the eyes see. Mirrors also reflect back our thoughts and our opinions of ourselves. These thoughts or opinions are much more important than our outward appearance.

Many of us have met people who are beautiful on the outside but believe that they are ugly, or people who are greatly loved by others but cannot love themselves. Our deepest thoughts are often reflections of our souls. Thoughts are a reflection of our love for ourselves, our egos, our dislike of ourselves, how we treat ourselves, and our overall self-opinion.

Money Doesn't Stay with People Who Don't Trust Themselves

Personal truths are often spoken in moments of peak emotion.

After explaining the CASHFLOW Quadrant to an individual or a group, I give them a moment to decide their next step. First, they decide which quadrant they are in right now. Next, I ask them which quadrant they would like to move to, if they need to move.

Some people look at me and say, "I'm happy exactly where I am."

Others say, "I'm not happy, but I am not willing to change or move at this time."

And then there are people who are unhappy where they are and know they need to do something immediately. People in this category often speak most clearly about their personal truths. They use words that reflect their opinions of themselves, words that reflect their soul. And that is why I say, "Personal truths are spoken at moments of peak emotion."

At these moments of truth, I often hear:

- "I can't do that. I can't move from S to B. Are you crazy? I have a wife and three kids to feed."

- "I can't do that. I can't wait five years before I get another paycheck."

- "Invest? You want me to lose all my money, don't you?"

- "I don't have any money to invest."

- "I need more information before I do anything."

- "I tried that before. It doesn't work."

- "I don't need to know how to read financial statements. I can get by."

- "I don't have to worry. I'm still young."

- "I'm not smart enough."

- "I would do it if I could find the right people to do it with me."

- "My husband would never go for it."

- "My wife would never understand."

- "What would my friends say?"

- "I'm too old."

- "I'm too young."

- "It's not worth it."

- "I'm not worth it."

All Words Are Mirrors

Personal truths are spoken at moments of peak emotion. All words are mirrors, for they reflect back some insight as to what people think about themselves, even though they may be speaking about someone else.

My Best Advice

For those of you who are ready to move from one quadrant to another, the most important advice I know to give you is to be very aware of your words. Be especially aware of the words that come from your heart, your stomach, and your soul. If you are going to make a change, you must be aware of the thoughts and words generated by your emotions. If you are not aware when your emotions are doing your thinking, you will never survive the journey. You will always hold yourself back. If you say, "My spouse will never understand," you are really saying more about yourself. You may be using your spouse as an excuse for your own inaction, or you might actually be saying, "I don't have the courage or communication skills to convey these new ideas." All words are mirrors that provide opportunities for you to look into your soul.

Or if you say, "I can't stop working and start my own business. I have a mortgage and a family to think about," you might really be saying, "I'm tired. I don't want to do anything more," or "I really don't want to learn anything more." These are personal truths.

Personal Truths Are Also Personal Lies

These are truths, and they are also lies. If you lie to yourself, your journey will never be completed. My best advice is to listen to your doubts, fears, and limiting thoughts, and then dig deeper for the real truth.

For example, if you say, "I'm tired, and I don't want to learn something new," that may be a truth, but it is also a lie. The real truth may be, "If I don't learn something new, I'll be even more tired." And even deeper than that, "The truth is, I love learning new things. I would love to learn something new and get excited about life again. Maybe whole new worlds would open to me." Once you can get to that point of the deeper truth, you may find a part of you that is powerful enough to help you change.

Our Journey

Before Kim and I could move forward, we had to be willing to live with the opinions and criticisms we each had about ourselves. We had to be willing to live with doubts, but not let them stop us. Occasionally, the pressure would get to the boiling point, and our self-criticisms would flare up. I would blame her for my doubts, and she would blame me for hers. But we both knew before starting out on this journey that the only thing we had to ultimately face was our own personal doubts, criticisms, and inadequacies. Our real job as husband and wife, business partners, and soul mates along this journey was to keep reminding each other that each of us was much more powerful than our individual doubts, pettiness, and inadequacies. In that process, we learned to trust ourselves more. The ultimate goal for us was more than to simply get rich. It was to learn to be trustworthy with ourselves, as well as with money.

Remember that the only person who determines the thoughts you choose to believe about yourself is you. So the reward from the journey is not only the freedom that money buys, but the trust you gain in yourself. My best advice is to prepare daily to be bigger than your smallness. In my opinion, the reason most people stop and turn back from their dreams is because the tiny person found inside each of us wields more power than our bigger person.

Even though you may not be good at everything, take time developing what you need to learn and your world will change rapidly. Never run from what you know you need to learn. Face your fears and doubts, and new worlds will open to you.

Take Action
Believe in yourself, and start today!

Chapter Eighteen
IN SUMMARY

---

*Begin building pipelines of cash flow
to support you and your family.*

Kim and I used these seven steps to move from being homeless to becoming financially free in a few short years. These seven steps helped us find our own financial Fast Track, and we continue to use them today. I trust they can assist you in charting your own course to financial freedom.

To do so, you must be true to yourself. If you are not yet a long-term investor, get yourself there as fast as you can. What does this mean? Sit down and map out a plan to get control of your spending habits. Minimize your debt and liabilities. Live within your means, and then expand your means. Find out how much money invested per month, for how many months, at a realistic rate of return it will take to reach your goals of retiring, creating cash flow, and gaining financial freedom.

Simply having a long-term plan that reduces your consumer debt while putting away a small amount of money regularly will give you a head start if you start early enough and keep an eye on what you are doing.

At this level, keep it simple. Don't get fancy.

The reason I introduced you to the CASHFLOW Quadrant, the five levels of investors, and my three types of investors is to offer you many glimpses into who you are, what your interests may be, and who you want to ultimately become. I like to believe that anyone can find their own unique path to the financial Fast Track, regardless of which quadrant they operate from.

Remember what I said previously: Your boss's job is to give you a job. It's your job to make yourself rich.

Are you ready to stop hauling water buckets and begin building pipelines of cash flow to support you, your family, and your lifestyle?

Minding your own business might be difficult and sometimes confusing, especially at first. There is a lot to learn, regardless of how much you already know. It is a lifelong process. But the good news is that the hardest part of the process is at the start. Once you make the commitment, life really does get easier and easier. Minding your business is not hard to do. It's just common sense.

About the Author
Robert Kiyosaki

Best known as the author of *Rich Dad Poor Dad*—the #1 personal finance book of all time—Robert Kiyosaki has challenged and changed the way tens of millions of people around the world think about money. He is an entrepreneur, educator, and investor who believes the world needs more entrepreneurs who will create jobs.

With perspectives on money and investing that often contradict conventional wisdom, Robert has earned an international reputation for straight talk, irreverence, and courage and has become a passionate and outspoken advocate for financial education.

Robert and Kim Kiyosaki are founders of The Rich Dad Company, a financial education company, and creators of the *CASHFLOW*® games. In 2013, the company will leverage the global success of the Rich Dad games in the launch of a new and breakthrough offering in mobile and online gaming.

Robert has been heralded as a visionary who has a gift for simplifying complex concepts—ideas related to money, investing, finance, and economics—and has shared his personal journey to financial freedom in ways that resonate with audiences of all ages and backgrounds. His core principles and messages—like "your house is not an asset" and "Invest for cash flow" and "savers are losers"—have ignited a firestorm of criticism and ridicule... only to have played out on the world economic stage over the past decade in ways that were both unsettling and prophetic.

His point of view is that "old" advice—go to college, get a good job, save money, get out of debt, invest for the long term, and diversify—

has become obsolete advice in today's fast-paced Information Age. His Rich Dad philosophies and messages challenge the status quo. His teachings encourage people to become financially educated and to take an active role in investing for their future.

The author of 19 books, including the international blockbuster

Rich Dad Poor Dad, Robert has been a featured guest with media outlets in every corner of the world—from CNN, the BBC, Fox News, Al Jazeera, GBTV and PBS, to *Larry King Live, Oprah, Peoples Daily, Sydney Morning Herald, The Doctors, Straits Times, Bloomberg, NPR, USA TODAY*, and hundreds of others—and his books have topped international bestsellers lists for more than a decade. He continues to teach and inspire audiences around the world.

His most recent books include *Unfair Advantage: The Power of Financial Education, Midas Touch*, the second book he has co-authored with Donald Trump, and *Why "A" Students Work for "C" Students*.

To learn more, visit RichDad.com

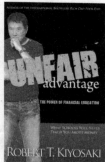